UNDER THE RUG

THE UNFORGETTABLE FORGOTTEN

L. Marie Williams
A Memoir

Privacy Information

The author tried to recreate events, locales and conversations from her memories of them. Conversations in the book all come from the author's recollection, though they are not written to represent word-for-word transcripts, the essence of the dialogue is accurate.

In order to maintain their anonymity and protect their privacy, in some instances, changes were made to identifying characteristics and details such as physical properties, occupations and places of residence. Some events have been condensed for literary purposes.

Dedication

This book is dedicated to the person that loved me even
when I didn't know how to love myself.
R.C.S.
I hope I made you proud. xo

PROLOGUE

I don't have a fairytale story to tell. There were no white picket fences during my childhood. No dog wagging its tail, waiting for me to come home from school or afternoon snacks before dinner. My life wasn't easy, but whose is? My dirty clothes and stringy dirty hair kept me from making friends easily. The kids and teachers at school did not really like me; in fact, most of them refuse to sit next to me in class because of the pungent piss odor coming from my chubby body. I tried desperately to hide it but in case you didn't know, piss is an awful smell and it's really difficult to mask that odor without showering and changing into clean clothes.

I essentially became the mean girl. I was always on the defense trying to protect my easily hurt feelings, but still trying to find a place to fit in. It was a lost cause. All the kids I went to school with would follow me from grade school to graduation. No matter what I did, my reputation as "pissy" could not be erased. Nevertheless, kids are kids, right? They couldn't understand the reasons behind my poor attitude and bad hygiene. They didn't know that I would rather go to school without showering, than wake mother. They wouldn't have cared that behind those sad, green eyes, I held some nasty secrets; secrets that I would carry with me for most of my life, until now.

1. AWAKENED

One of my first real memories as a child is imprinted so intensely in my mind that I can still smell the wet piss in my nose as my mother, Claudia, woke me up out of a deep sleep grabbing my hair and twisting it in her hands. She lifted me off the wet-carpeted, floor in my little sister's bedroom and slammed my head into both the dressers I was sleeping in between. Screaming, she smashed my face into the carpet like a dog.

"Smell it! Smell that nasty shit you little bitch! You are a fucking animal so I'm going to treat you like one! You like that shit, huh?" She yelled, as she drug me by hair out into the hallway. She slammed my head against the heavy, wood door and knocked all the air from my lungs with a hard kick to the stomach.

I cried out and begged her to stop... she didn't. She just kept kicking and punching me while I laid on the floor, curled into a ball trying to protect my face. I could feel her getting tired and I thought she would stop. My head was throbbing in pain, I just wanted to go get dressed as fast as I could and go to school so I could get away from

6

her.

She grabbed two handfuls of my hair and pulled me across the floor near the kitchen to the side entrance of our house.

"Get the fuck out of my house! You want to be a nasty little bitch then you can go to school just like that!"

The tears streamed down my face, but I got up and walked down the five steps to the door. I hesitated to open it, but I did. I turned to her and begged her not to make me leave. My cries were ignored. She punched me in the back of the head one last time and pushed me out the door, locking it behind me.

I stood there, in the driveway, with snow under my bare feet, crying. I thought of running away and never coming back, but where would I go? Who would help me? I couldn't go to school like that. I shivered as the wind blew. My tears stuck to my swollen face and my black sweat pants felt heavy and cold. My school was 15 minutes away and I was out of options.

I heard my next-door neighbors making noise in their house. They had a daughter my age and another one a few years older. For most of my time living next to them, we didn't like each other; we played together out of convenience rather than actual friendship.

I was scared to knock on the door but the wind forced my hand. Her mother greeted me and the minute I saw her face I couldn't hold back my sobs. My secret was out for them to judge me as harshly as my mother had. I was thoroughly embarrassed.

Brandy stood in the living room with a look of pity on her face as I explained what happened to me. I could tell in that moment that she felt bad for ever making me the butt of her endless jokes.

Her mom ordered them to take me upstairs and find something for me to wear. I took a hot shower and dressed in a pair of jogging pants and a turtleneck. Carol Ann, Brandy's older sister, had even given me a pair of Skippy's to wear that were a size to big and a jacket to put on so I would be warm.

In the car, on the way to school, I cried silently as I looked out the window but by the time we pulled up to the school, I cleaned my face and prepared myself.

My daddy was gone but I always prayed that he would come and rescue me from my mother one day. My prayers went unanswered and most nights I cried myself to sleep in silent tears so no one could hear me.

Every morning I tried to wake up before her just to hide evidence of the night before. My mom made me bathe at night so showering before school was a dead giveaway that I had peed on myself while I was asleep. I preferred to be the target of the childish jokes from my classmates and teachers as they held their nose when I passed by them in class than to let Claudia find out about my accidents.

I began to hate myself. *Why couldn't I be like all the other kids at school?* My body betrayed me when all I wanted, so badly, was to have control over my bladder. During the day, I had no trouble holding it if I needed too. *Why was it so difficult to do at night?* I could not understand. I prayed about it every night; I even stopped drinking water two hours before bed but nothing helped.

The anger in my heart grew deeper each time I looked up at my little sister, Vanessa, sleeping peacefully and snuggled in her oversized bed while I lay on the floor in a sleeping bag beside her, in between the two dressers. I was jealous and becoming resentful. *Why was she so special? What did she do, that was so great, that made my mother love her so much? Why couldn't I be more like her? Why didn't my mother love me?*

Vanessa was my mother's pride and joy. Maybe it was because we had different fathers and she was engaged to be married to Vanessa's dad. Maybe it was because her father was white and had a good job and my father was never around. No matter the reason, all I wanted was for her to love me the way she loved my sister. I needed it like I needed the air I breathed.

***

I stared out the window of the top bunk bed while my little cousin Derrick slept at my feet. I was praying not to pee in the bed and avoid the embarrassing moment of watching my uncle and all his friends laughing at me. Not to mention the fact that I know Derrick was scared because he didn't want to wake up wet, but he was forced to sleep in the bed with me.

I was visiting my Aunt Camilla's house for the weekend. She was my mother's older sister. I liked going over there to get away from my mom and play with all my cousins. My Aunt Camilla had four kids and always had a house full of people. She was much more laid back compared to my stern mother. That night she let my uncle Thomas have a bunch of his teenage friends stay the night for a sleepover in the attack.

One friend in-particular, took an unusual interest in me while everyone else seemed to be distracted with video games and wrestling. His seventeen-year-old frame was muscular and strong with pale white skin and sandy blonde hair. He looked like he could model for a magazine ad.

Before my aunt sent my cousin and me to bed, he grabbed me on the stairs and kissed me. *My first kiss.* His mouth was wet and his teeth bit my bottom lip with aggressive gentleness. His affection felt good and inside I was screaming with excitement. Someone actually liked me... *A boy!* Before he disappeared upstairs, he called out to me. I turned back to look at him and he threw down piece of black, sheer, lingerie that belonged to my aunt. I picked it up and looked at it with puzzlement. I could tell it was way too big to fit my boyish seven-year-old frame.

"Put that on, I'll come down and see you later." He demanded in a whisper.

I was unable to go to sleep because it was loud upstairs. The boys were making noise and the bathroom light was shining on me through the open door. I was scared to wake up wet in front of the only boy who had ever shown me any attention. I left the lingerie hanging on the handle of the attack door so I could return it to wherever he had gotten it from in the morning. I was worried that he would be mad at me for opting not to put it on and staying in my comfortable pajamas. *What if he doesn't like me anymore?*

My eyes grew heavy and I fell asleep. When I woke up, the whole house was silent and darkness filled the room with only a nearby streetlight on, peering through the bedroom window. He was on top of me stroking my face. I began to panic feeling the bed for wetness only to find that my pajamas were off. I was in the sheer, black lingerie piece that he had thrown down to me earlier. I was uncomfortable seeing him there when I opened my eyes but he hushed my voice by putting his finger over my mouth. I thought I was dreaming. He ran his other hand over my flat chest, down my stomach and over my virgin vagina.

I looked down at my sleeping cousin with whom I shared the bed with and felt conflicted. A part of me hoped that he would wake up and the other part of me was scared of the trouble I would be in if he did. I laid there stiff and let him touch me while I wondered where he had put my pajamas. I was trying to feel for them but they weren't within my reach. I wondered how he was able to move me and take my clothes off me without waking me up. Again, I felt betrayed by my own body for not waking up before he had taken off my clothes. I was embarrassed that a boy I liked had seen my body, naked. I tried to cover myself with my arms but he wouldn't let me. *Why did he want to see me naked? Why was he making me feel so uncomfortable? Why couldn't he kiss me with my own clothes on?* There was so much that I did not understand. His touch made awakened a sensation in my body that I had never felt before. I couldn't speak; I was frozen in the moment. When he finished, and climbed down off the bunk bed, I grabbed the blanket. "You can't tell anyone that we did this because we will get in a lot of trouble, okay?" He reasoned. I nodded hesitantly and he disappeared through the attack door and back upstairs.

I found my pajamas, went to the bathroom and changed back into my clothes. I went over the events in my head, still confused about what happened. I had never been touched in those places before. It felt strange but good. I didn't want it to feel good. I wanted him to stop because I did not feel comfortable having him see my body. *Does this mean that he likes me?* He was right, if I told my mom, I was sure to get in

11

trouble. I was not supposed to like boys and certainly was not supposed to be naked in front on any of them. I would never tell...*Ever!*

2. SECRETS

A short time passed and things got progressively worse at home. My mom could not take it anymore. She was tired of fighting with my sister's dad about me. She told me that she needed a break and I was going to live with my grandmother in Kentucky for a while. *Why do you need a break from me but Vanessa gets to stay here with you?*

We rode the greyhound in from Ohio to Kentucky in silence. I held back tears because I did not want her to see me weak. I learned quickly that crying in front of my mother only made her feel more powerful. When we arrived at the house, it was dark outside. It was foreign to me and so were the people inside.

I could tell that my mom was disgusted by the conditions of the house. The moment we stepped onto the front porch the stench hit us in the face like a fastball pitch. Once inside, her face tightened, trying to shield her nose from the pungent smell of dog shit and rotting food. Under our feet, shielded by our shoes, the carpet was hard as rocks; it was as if we were walking on gravel. She was tired but I could tell that she was afraid to sit down anywhere let alone, sleep in the bed they offered.

The grandmother that she was delivering me to was a stranger to me. She lived there with her husband Boone and their son, David. He was my mother's half- brother and was only a few years older than I was. My mom was all I knew and I prayed that she would not leave me there with those strange people.

The next morning, she began her cleaning adventure. The bathtub was filled with piss and shit from the small petting zoo that my grandmother kept in her house. My mother washed the mound of month-old dishes left in the sink, cleaned the kitchen floors, countertops and the stove that had grease so thick on top of it that it looked as though you could fry an egg right there without a pan. By the time she finished she was dog-tired and although the house was not clean by her standards, she was satisfied with her progress.

She stayed a few days and it was peaceful between us. It was the first time that I had spent any time real one-on-one time with her and we felt close. Maybe it was because I was the only familiar face to her as well or maybe it was because my sister and her dad were not there. Nevertheless, I enjoyed the moment and I clung to her. I took the opportunity to admire her beauty. My mother was mesmerizing. Her hair was as dark as coal against her fair completion. She was tall by my standards with a small frame and wide, childbearing, hips. Her style was classy and she always smelled something like heaven to me, but it was her light hazel eyes that sealed the deal and I prayed I would, one day, be as beautiful as she.

It was so early that it was still dark outside when we woke up. I knew she was leaving but I was still holding on to hope that she would reconsider and take me home with her. I did not want to stay with those strange people in that unfamiliar, dirty place. She hugged me and kissed my forehead.

"Be good." She said and she turned to walk away

"Mommy, don't leave me!" I screamed.

I tried to hold it in but I couldn't help it. I felt like my heart was being ripped from my chest. I latched onto her leg for dear life as she walked out the door. I begged her, "Please don't leave me, Mommy! I will be good. I won't pee in the bed anymore!" She peeled my fingers away one by one until I lost my grip. I could see the sadness etched across her face as she turned and walked towards the car. I kicked and screamed on the gravel-carpet floor until I was completely exhausted. My grandmother tried to comfort me but it was of no use. I wanted my mom. I could not believe she left me. I was alone and afraid. *Will she ever come back for me?*

As time went on and I knew that she was not coming back, I got to know the strangers I was living with. My estranged family became my only family. Eventually, I learned to love them but my heart was irrevocably broken.

My grandmother was a sweet, little, old woman. She would give the shirt off her back to a complete-stranger, but she was a hoarder. She hoarded animals and junk which is why her house was always filthy. She rarely cleaned anything, including herself. She covered dirty things up with more dirty things. Her parents gave her the house we lived in so she didn't have work.

Grandma's husband Boone was an alcoholic who worked a lot and occasionally hit on her when he was drunk. He rarely took a shower and wore the same dirty clothes all the time. Then there was my uncle David. He was barely ten years old but he was something like the man of the house and hardly got in trouble for anything.

My grandmother was a pushover, but there was a fire inside of her and I would see it on occasion when we were punished. She would make us go outside and pick our own switch from the tree in the front yard but her whooping's were nothing compared to Claudia's. My grandmother had control over herself and disciplining us was not something she enjoyed or did often.

In the beginning, David and I hated one another. We played together but he did not like me always following him and his friends around. He once told me that his best friend, Al, didn't like me and trying to seem cool, I called him a bitch. David went back and told him what I said and when my grandmother made me go get David from Al's house one day, he stood there and let his friend punch me in the face. They laughed hysterically as I cried and ran home to tell my grandmother what happened.

My face was dripping blood and tears as I snitched on them. When David walked in the house for dinner, she beat him with a wooden spoon as I stood there holding a towel to my nose, trying not to laugh out loud as he cried out in pain. He felt no loyalty towards the stranger-niece that invaded his life and for a long time, I didn't either.

***

Summer turned into winter and back to summer again. The house was filthy as ever and it didn't help that my uncle David and I would throw our unwanted food on the floor behind the refrigerator so my grandmother would not catch us being wasteful with our vegetables. I guess I figured that the dogs would eat them. She never caught us and if she did, she never said anything.

Over time, my uncle and I had become close, like brother and sister. We pretty much spent all our free time together on adventures in the small town we lived in. We went swimming in the nearby river, played dodge ball and freeze tag. We even found an abandoned train station once and we pretended to ride the train into other made-up places. He taught me how to do a cartwheel and we made an indoor tent in our shared bedroom out of blankets. At night, we would stay up together watching television or playing video games.

One night after my grandmother went to sleep; David and I were up watching T.V., as usual. He looked at me so excited, "Look what I found!" He got up off the bed, picked up a VHS tape and put it in the VCR. He turned the volume down low and the T.V. lit up with two naked people on the screen, having sex.

"Yuck! David, turn it off!" I screamed at him.

"Shh! It's my dad's! Just watch." He said, towering over me while I sat on the edge of the bed.

He began rubbing my shoulder and put his hands down my shirt onto my flat chest. My body froze. I felt uncomfortable watching the people on the screen have sex and more uncomfortable that my uncle David was touching me. I was ashamed that my hidden place was getting moist and my small nipples were poking out. My body was defying my command to be unbothered.

I watched as his shorts poked out in front of me. He used his free hand to pull himself out of his shorts and he stood in front of me tugging at his erect penis. I moved away when I saw it, releasing his hand from body. He came closer to me.

"David, STOP! That's nasty." I yelled at him.

"Shhh! You're going to wake my Mom up. It's just a dick! I'm not going to hurt you. It feels good, doesn't it? Let me show you or I'm gonna tell my mom you've been throwing food behind the fridge and you're gonna get in trouble!" He warned.

I just sat there, still. He grabbed my hand and I closed my eyes as he placed it on his small penis.

"Just rub it up and down, like this." He showed me.

He lifted my shirt and started rubbing my flat chest. Suddenly, I felt wetness on my fingertips. I stopped and pushed him away from me.

"Yuck! What is that?" I asked, looking down at my hand with disgust.

"It's just cum. That means you're doing a good job." He encouraged.

"I gotta pee. Turn this off!" I demanded as I turned and walked away into the connecting bathroom.

"Marie, if you tell anyone, we're both gonna get in trouble!" He said behind me.

"I'm not gonna tell!" I said and shut the bathroom door.

Afterwards, the touching became more frequent, as if it was regular activity when the day turned into night and the house fell silent.

I began thinking it was normal for us. Even though, I felt sick to my stomach after each time it happened, I never stopped it or told a soul. He never penetrated my body and for that reason, I made exceptions for it. I don't believe either of us understood the gravity of what we were doing or how it would affect our lives.

Walking home one day, I noticed an unfamiliar car parked in the driveway. I was puzzled because in the small town we lived in, we rarely had visitors that drove to our house. When I ran inside to see who it was, she was standing there looking like an angel. Her sun-kissed skin glistened. I ran to her and hugged her tightly; I never wanted to let go. I thought I was dreaming. I had forgotten how good her Tommy Hilfiger perfume smelled mixed with the natural odors of her body. My mom had come back for me.

Of course, she immediately made me take a bath. She sat on the edge of my bed and combed my matted hair into two pigtails. I tried not to cry as I felt the warmth of her touch against my flesh. I missed her so much. I dreamed about her every night and as much as I hated her for leaving me, I loved her so deeply in that moment. The mere sight of her alone was enough to erase all my pain.

3. HOME

The drive back to home to Ohio was blissful. I was so thankful that she came back for me. I told her about my time in Kentucky but I never told her my secret. I loved her so much and I wanted us to stay in the moment forever. I knew that telling her would only make her angry with me and I did not want to disappoint her. I finally had my mom back.

Once we reached Ohio, life seemed to continue as if I had never left. The good days were over within weeks and I was back to sleeping on the floor, in my little sister's bedroom as if nothing had changed at all. I was still peeing in the "bed" and hiding it from my mother, although this time she began finding my soiled underwear in the trash can. She put an end to that with a few punches to the head and whelps on my back.

I had to find a new resolution to my problem so I began throwing my soiled underwear behind the dressers or any place that I didn't think she would look, as I had with my unwanted food when I lived with my grandma. She quickly caught on to that trick due to the foul- smelling odor in the house. She turned the room I shared with my sister, upside down, trying to find the location of the horrible smell. Once she found my secret hiding place, hell had no fury like Claudia. Her tongue cut right through me when she told me that she was not going to continue to punish my little sister by forcing her to share "HER" room with me... as if sleeping on the floor next to my sister's queen size bed was a privilege. I felt so small and unwelcomed; I just stood there crying as she spoke.

"Starting tonight, you're going to sleep in the basement. That is going to be your new room." My mother informed me.

That night, just as my mom said, my sister's dad walked me downstairs and showed me my new "bedroom". A twin-size mattress, covered in plastic, was on the cold, concrete, floor. He gave me a pillow and my usual sleeping bag then turned off the light and returned upstairs.

I was alone. I laid there with my eyes open, listening to the sound of dripping water and floors creaking from them walking around upstairs. I was so scared to go to sleep. He left a small light on for me, over the sink. It made shadows against the wall that scared me even more. I thought of the bugs that must have been down in the dungeon-like basement and I cringed with intense fear. I stayed awake until I could not fight my sleep any longer and I gave in.

***

Visiting my aunt's house one day, my mom called me downstairs into the kitchen. I thought I was in trouble because adults surrounded the table and everyone had a serious look on their face. I was scared.

"Marie, I'm going to ask you some questions and I need you to be honest with me, okay?" My aunt Camilla asked.

"Okay."

"Do you remember staying the night here the night of your uncle's party, when all those boys were here?" She questioned.

"Yes." I responded, timidly.

"Did one of those boys touch you?"

My eyes widened. *How could you know that? Why are you asking me this in front of my mom? Oh my God, she is going to kill me.*

"No, Titi." I lied.

"Marie, don't lie to me! You are not going to get in trouble. Derrick told us that he saw one of the boys on top of you. Please tell me the truth." She begged.

They called my cousin Derrick downstairs and he told them what he saw.

Why is he telling them? Doesn't he know how bad my mom is going to beat me? She is going to be so mad!

I was beyond scared so I kept lying. Finally, I gave up. I told them that the boy had touched me but I was so embarrassed that I refused to give them all the details. Moreover, I never wanted to get the boy in trouble. He seemed nice and he didn't hurt me.

My mom did not seem angry with me for finally coming out and telling the truth, in fact, it was the opposite. She had tears in her eyes and I could tell that it was hard for her to talk. I never saw her cry over me and I felt like someone was stabbing me in the chest seeing her in pain. I did not know why she was hurting but I wanted to hug her and tell her that everything was going to be okay. It made me feel good that I told her the truth, but they wanted more details than I was able to give them.

I couldn't tell her that I was confused about the whole thing or that I thought he liked me and that's why he was touching me. I could not tell her that I was uncomfortable when I woke up and realized that he changed my clothes or that I wanted him to stop but the feeling of his touch was unlike anything I had ever felt before and a part of me liked it. I could not tell her that it felt good to me to have someone touch me in a way that was not causing me physical pain. I couldn't tell her any of that; I didn't even understand it enough to express it. I wanted them to let it go, it seemed like every day someone was asking me questions about what happened to me. I made up my mind that I didn't want anything bad to happen to him so I would lie. No matter what, no one could know the truth.

Just when the questions started to die down a little bit my dad showed up out of nowhere, as my mother and I were getting ready to leave the house one day after school. He pulled his big, green truck into our driveway.

I was so happy to see him. I hoped he would take me with him but to my dismay, he just wanted to talk. I knew exactly what he wanted to discuss and I did not want to talk about it with anyone, especially not my father. I was so embarrassed that he knew. I did not want him to look at me differently or be angry with me.

We sat in his truck. He fought back tears and asked me what happened; yet another person wanting me to explain a situation that I did not understand myself. When I went silent for too long he began carrying the conversation.

"Marie, I need you to tell me what he did to you. If he touched you, I need to know. I promise you won't be in trouble, but him..."

Tears fell down his cheeks and his voice cut out. He hit his fist against the steering wheel in anger.

"I'm going to pick up my brothers and go find him. I'm going to kill him and bury him on my dad's land. Just tell me what happened baby girl, please?" He pleaded with me.

I began crying. Seeing my father hurting and so torn up inside made it hard for me to breathe. I wanted to take away his pain and tell him the truth, but... *What if he kills him? He's going to go to jail and I'll never see him again.* I couldn't tell him. He continued to beg me and for the first time I looked at my father in his eyes and lied to him. I did it to save myself from the embarrassment and to keep him from killing the boy, or worse, going to prison for doing it.

"Dad, nothing happened." I lied.

My mom came out of the house and went to her car. My dad met her there and they exchanged words I couldn't hear from the inside of the truck. My mom waved me to come on, I hugged my dad and he kissed me goodbye, on the cheek. I got in the backseat of my mom's car. As soon as he was out of the driveway, she turned and punched me in the face.

"You lying, little, bitch! He's right, that boy probably didn't

24

fucking touch you!" She screamed at me.

I held my face and tried to hold in my cries. He left me again and all I could feel was loneliness and longing for him to come back and save me.

4. SAFETY

My aunt Nicole was visiting our house with her husband and infant son. She was my mother's youngest sister but her maturity and caring nature was well beyond her years.

Everyone was laughing and having a good time socializing. I enjoyed having people visit because it cut the tension in the house and gave my mother something else to focus that wasn't me, which left me time to play freely with my little sister Vanessa and my new baby cousin.

Bedtime was looming over me like a rain cloud and I knew that I would be forced down into the dungeon. I tried not to think about it, but I kept watching the clock hoping that my mother was too preoccupied to notice the time. I thought that if I stayed quiet she would forget I was there and let me stay up longer or at least until my aunt and uncle left... I was wrong.

When she told me it was bedtime, I sat in the stairwell leading to the basement and cried. I begged her to let me stay up just a little while longer but she refused so my cries became a full out tantrum. I screamed and kicked in the stairwell begging her through tears until she sprinted towards me like a tornado down the stairs with a belt in her hand, swinging it full force against my skin. Normally, I would have covered myself in the fetal position and tried to hush my cries as she hit me but I had an audience so I let it all out. I did not hide my painful cries. I screamed out in agony every time the belt hit my skin.

My aunt Nicole called out to my mom and begged her to stop but that only pissed her off more. She hit me one last time with the belt and walked away. I could hear her yelling at my aunt.

"Don't you ever tell me what the fuck to do with my own child!" She screamed.

I heard the front door slam and I crawled down stairs and laid on my pitiful, plastic mattress, sobbing into my pillow. My skin was on fire, red and welted. I thought about what had just happened and I was scared. *As soon as she leaves, she is going to come down here and kill me!* I continued crying.

There was an unfamiliar voice at the top of the steps calling my name.

"Marie, can you come up here please."

Hesitantly, I walked up the stairs and was escorted outside to the front yard by a police officer. There was so much noise and commotion going on, my neighbors were outside and everyone was yelling. I couldn't focus. An officer asked me to show him all my marks and bruises. With his flashlight pointed at me, I did. He seemed to be writing each one down on a notepad. Moments later, after speaking with another officer, he came and told me to get in the backseat of my aunt's car and that I was going to be spending the night with her. Relief instantly came over me, but I was still very scared. I told a secret that I was not supposed to tell and I knew my mom was outraged, so whenever they sent me back home with her, she was surely to make me pay for it.

One night turned into a couple of months and I didn't mind at all. My aunt Nicole was the manager of a movie theatre and sometimes I got to go to work with her. I would sit and watch movies all day long, I got lost in them. The staff watched out for me and my aunt always knew where I was, she would check on me during her breaks. I wished that my mom was more like her. She was patient with me, even when I had an accident in bed. I would wake up scared to tell her and try to hide the evidence but when she found it, she never punished me for it. She simply told me not to hide it from her so she could make sure it was cleaned up properly and I took a bath.

When my mom finally married Peter, my sister's dad, I was not a part of the wedding but I did attend as a guest. I did not get to sit at the special table, wear a pretty dress and walk down the aisle throwing flowers. I did not get to ride in the limo or have my name called over the microphone as the D.J. announced the wedding party. I was dressed in a blue and white skater dress with my hair in pigtails. I watched just like everyone else as my mother and Peter were married and I was out casted. I tried to conceal my sadness and jealousy at how happy they looked as a family because I was no longer there to burden them.

After the wedding, Claudia began getting visitation days with me. She questioned me about my aunt's house and wanted to know what it was like living there. She seemed bitter and angry with my aunt for calling the police on her. She always brought it up during our visits and manipulated me into giving her information. I was intimidated and I thought that the only way to get back into good graces with my mother was to agree with everything she said, even when she talked bad about my aunt who saved me from her wrath. Despite all that she had done, I still craved her love and affection like a drug.

Upon my return from a visit with my mom, I told my aunt Nicole about the things my mother said and my young aunt had enough. Standing up against Claudia was a big deal for anyone in our family to begin with and she was tired of fighting with her sister, so she decided to send me back to my mother.

After talking to my mom on the phone, my aunt stormed into my room and told me that my mom would be picking me up in a few hours to take me back to Kentucky to live with my grandmother again. I begged her to let me stay but her mind was made up. She was tired of the hurricane of drama. It was time for me to go.

I called the only person that I knew who could possibly reach my dad. I wanted to say goodbye to him one last time because I knew that once I got to Kentucky, I was never coming back.

My uncle Angelo was my dad's older brother and the only number that I knew by heart for anyone on my dad's side of the family. He picked up the phone by nothing short of a miracle. I fought back tears long enough to explain to him what was happening.

"Wait by the phone. I'm going to call you right back."

"Okay, Tio." I replied, anxiously.

As I waited for him, I thought about how hard it would be for me to say goodbye to my dad. Even though I rarely saw him, to me, he was everything. I built him up to be the hero who would, one day, rescue me from all the madness in my life.

Two hours later, my dad and my uncle knocked at the front door of my aunt's apartment. I hugged him so tight; I thought I was going to burst. They talked with my aunt for a moment, grabbed the garbage bag full of my clothes and took me with them.

5. NEW LIFE

We lived upstairs in a three-bedroom duplex apartment he rented in a hurry from one of his friends. Living with my dad was a major adjustment for both of us. He was used to being single, only responsible for himself, and I was used to living in fear that nothing in my life was permanent.

He was a stranger to me. We shared the same DNA but we didn't know much about one another or how to live together as a family. I didn't know if I could trust him or how long it would last but I decided to enjoy having him around no matter how short the time was.

His rules and punishments were different. Somehow, he eventually knocked down my walls and I felt safe with him. I began to believe in his love for me and I could see the guilt he felt for not saving me sooner. As I became acclimated to life with him, our bond grew stronger and more powerful than any love I had ever felt up to that point in my life. It became us against the world. He was my biggest supporter and he was always very blunt with me; constantly teaching me life lessons beyond my third-grade comprehension.

He worked as a forklift operator by trade but he did odd jobs whenever the opportunity presented itself. He didn't have a car so he rode a bicycle to and from work every day, regardless if it was seventy degrees or below zero outside. We lived below poverty level. It was always a struggle to make sure there was food on the table but somehow, he always found a way.

I still peed in the bed and I still did my best to hide it, even though he never raised his hand to me in anger or frustration. When he figured out that I was hiding it, he wasn't angry, he did his best not to make me feel bad about it and tried to show me how to clean up after myself by washing my underwear in the sink and hanging them to dry. I still felt disappointed and embarrassed that I could not control my bladder while I slept.

I spent every weekend at my mom's house and to me it seemed like a vacation with cable television. Living with my dad made me feel safer being around my mom. I finally had someone who would stick up for me at any given moment if I didn't feel safe. With one phone call, he would come running to my defense.

My dad was barely able to afford the household bills but every time he was paid and there was a little extra left over, we always did something fun like make homemade root beer floats and rent movies to watch together.

One Friday after school, I packed my bag, ready to go to my mom's house for the weekend but she never showed up. I called and called but didn't get an answer. I left voicemails, crying on the phone and my dad watched as I sat feeling disappointed and abandoned. When she finally returned my call, my dad stood in the kitchen listening to my side of the conversation.

"Marie, I'm not coming to get you this weekend."

"Why not?"

"I don't think I should be forced to take you every weekend while your dad gets to be out partying! I need a weekend to myself." She explained.

"But you have Vanessa?" I reminded her.

"Give me the phone!" My dad demanded. "What's the problem, Claudia?" He asked.

I couldn't hear what my mom was saying but my dad looked at me with a stern face as I wiped the tears from my cheeks. I could see fire in his eyes.

"What the fuck do you mean every other weekend? I don't ask you for shit and the only time you see her is on the weekends!" He pressed.

My mom screamed something into the phone causing my dad to pull it from his ear and she hung up.

I ran in my room and lay across the bed. I sobbed into my pillow. He followed behind me and kneeled at the edge of my bed rubbing my back.

"Dad, why doesn't she love me?"

He looked shocked and hurt by my question. I could tell he was fighting it but tears swelled in his eyes and streamed down his face. I knew my pain was stabbing him like a knife to the heart.

"Baby, I don't know. But it's her loss!"

I hugged him and he held me in that embrace for several

minutes

"I love you, Marie."

"I love you too, Dad!"

Before he left my room, I asked, "Dad, will you show me how to pray?" He kneeled down next to my bed and I knelt beside him.

"Put your hands together like this." He instructed.

After our prayer, he let me sleep in his bed with him and it was the first time that my body did not betray me. I felt completely safe with my dad.

6. Down Hill

Before I went to live with my father, he had a reputation for heavy partying but that slowed down drastically. I knew he drank but he never did any drugs in front of me.

At eight years old, I thought my dad was Superman. He never had to hit me to get me to do as he asked. Occasionally, he would slap me in the back of the head and make my ears ring with his heavy hands; however, his words and tough demeanor were enough to make me move. When I would be put on punishment for something I did wrong, he stuck to it. Our relationship was solidified. It was us against the world... Until...

Her name was Leah. She set her eyes on my dad and was determined to win him over despite the fact that she was not his type. She saw his weakness in me and she exploited it. The lack of female presence in my life made me cling to her and my father was happy for me to have a woman to look up too. I began spending time with her almost every day. She took me shopping and showed me how to comb my hair. For the first time, I was going to school with new, clean, clothes. She took a special interest in me and treated me as if I was her daughter. I soon began my own campaign with my father to get them together but he resisted.

Her tall, tiny, frame and pale white skin was not appealing to him. I knew that he would have to get to know her better in-order to see past that because she was not exotic looking like the women he was used to dating.

Months passed and they began spending more and more time together because of me. She began buying him expensive gifts, inviting us places and bringing us food. Before I knew it, they were spending time together even when I was not around. When they came out openly to me about having a relationship together, I was initially excited. I felt like I had a family for the first time.

It was not long after that, that my dad lost his job and we had to move in with her. Things began to change rapidly. My relationship with my dad began to strain. He slept all day and was up all night, partying. He was always moody and barely spent any time with me at all. The house was usually dark and I was forbidden from knocking on their bedroom door to wake them unless it was an emergency. Most days, when I was not in school or at my mom's house, I busied myself with Leah's insane movie collection. I began to resent him for not being present and creating a distance between us. He started to become a shell of the man that I had grown to love and admire.

Leah stopped spending time with me too. Her entire focus was my dad. She started telling him stories about me and twisting my words to get me in trouble with him. That took a major toll on our relationship. I began to hate her for coming into our lives and stealing the only thing that I had left, my father's love.

My mom divorced Peter and she was working two jobs to make ends meet. Before they split for good, she had my youngest sister, Avery, and needed my help babysitting so I began spending more and more time at my mother's house.

I'm not sure if my dad cared much because he was so self-involved that I think it made it easier for him that I was not around much. The tension in the house between Leah and me had gotten so thick you could cut it with a knife. She was always over dramatizing the smallest things and putting ideas in his head to diminish his perception of me as his little girl.

Once I figured out what she was doing, I could barely speak a full sentence to her without being sarcastic or flat out disrespectful. I tried to bite my tongue out of respect for my dad, but she made it increasingly difficult.

With free time on my hands that summer and no parental eyes watching over me, I started to show out. I was still a pre-teen but grown men started to notice my over-developing body and I enjoyed the attention. It felt good to be noticed. I started smoking my mom's cigarettes and hanging out with the wrong crowd of people. I even, secretly, had a boyfriend and lost my virginity.

My dad's lack of interest in me caused me to start being sloppy and forgetting to cover my tracks. One day he stopped to check on me unexpectedly, while my mom was at work. My boyfriend was visiting me at the same time. My dad did not find him in the house because he jumped off the apartment balcony but he knew something wasn't right and went ballistic. He made an emergency call to my mom at work and made her come home early. He questioned me a thousand times wanting to know if I was having sex and I continued to lie. I told him no but my mom made him leave the room so she could talk to me. She said, "Marie, if you're having sex then we need to know so we can put you on birth control. Once we take you to the doctor, they are gonna be able to tell us if you've done it before so you might as well come clean now." I started to cry and that was all the response she needed to know the truth.

I begged her not to tell my dad but the good-cop, bad-cop routine worked. When he came back in the house, she made me tell him. I watched as my father's eyes filled with tears of anger and disappointment. He spewed insults at me calling me "a little hoe." He forced me to pack my things and told me that I was going home with him. He blamed my mother for my actions because she wasn't there enough to watch over me. I begged him not take me but he wasn't hearing anything I had to say.

Once we got home, he grounded me to my room, upstairs. I was not allowed to use the phone, watch television or come down stairs other than to use the restroom.

That first night, he and Leah came into my room to talk to me. They were looking for details. Where did it happen? Did I use protection? How many times? The more answers I gave the more the tears fell from my father's eyes. Seeing him hurt, broke my heart, but deeper than that, I could see his disappointment. When he walked out of my bedroom that night, our relationship was forever changed. Leah tried to seem understanding and said she would try to reason with my father but I knew better.

As the days passed by, my father's heart hardened towards me. I would try to talk to him whenever he brought my food up to my room and he wouldn't even look at me. Leah did not help my cause either. She took every opportunity to fuel my father's anger towards me. Any time he allowed me to come downstairs and include me in dinner; she made it her business to remind him of my punishment. When I was allowed to take a bath, she would pick at me in front of him and complain that I was taking too long in an attempt to be out of my room longer. As a result, my dad enforced a new rule of one bath a week. I knew that she was finally getting exactly what she wanted. I played right into her hand.

One afternoon, I was bringing my lunch plates downstairs to be washed when she stopped me at the bottom of the steps.

"Where do you think you're going?" She demanded.

"I'm going to put my dishes in the sink like my dad told me too." I replied.

"Your dad didn't tell you that you could come down the steps! You can leave them there and I'll get them." She spat.

"Whatever, bitch." I mumbled under my breath.

"What the fuck did you just say to me? Did you just call me a bitch?" She asked.

My frustration was at an all-time high with her and my anger got the best of me. There was a dirty coffee cup on the steps from my lunch dishes.

"I didn't say shit to you! You always wanna put on a show to try to get me in trouble! Here!" I swiftly flung the coffee cup hard at her chest. She caught it but her face dropped and she yelled for my dad.

"You better get this little bitch right now before I hurt her!" She screamed.

Before I could say anything else my dad whisked up the steps, grabbed me by my throat and carried me to the top. He slammed me against the wall like a rag doll. I could barely breathe as my body dangled in the air, unable to touch the ground. He headbutted me and we touched nose to nose. In his anger, he spat in my face with every word from his mouth.

"Don't you ever raise your fucking voice or put your hands on her again! I will fucking kill you! Do you hear me you little whore?"

I could not make a sound but tears streamed down my face as I saw the seriousness in his glossy eyes. He dropped me on the ground breaking my gold, nameplate, necklace upon his release. He walked back downstairs and slammed the door that led to the stairway behind him. I laid in the same spot for hours, silently crying. Hatred brewed inside of me for the woman that I had once looked up too like a mother.

The following morning my father came into my room with an empty, tan, mop bucket.
"There won't be any more of you coming downstairs! If you need to use the bathroom, use this and when it gets full, you can come down stairs and empty it. Otherwise, I don't wanna fucking see you!" He commanded, exasperated, as he walked out of my room and slammed the door.

Days began running into each other and I tried to find ways to busy myself and keep my mind occupied. Sometimes, I stared out my bedroom window and watched the neighborhood kids play outside. I couldn't talk to anyone out of my window because even if no one was home, the next-door neighbors were my dad's friends and they had their eye on me. My boyfriend was long gone and only a memory. I was not even able sneak and talk on the phone because I couldn't go downstairs. My dad booby-trapped the door at the bottom of the stairs, so if I even tried to turn the handle on the door, he knew and there was hell to pay. I was trapped in the four walls of my homemade prison with nothing but my own thoughts and a bucket to use the bathroom in.

One day, while cleaning out some old boxes, I found books that Leah had stored away and asked her if I could read one of them. She agreed. The book that stood out to me more than anything was called, "I Know Why the Caged Bird Sings" by Maya Angelou.

I instantly became fascinated with her story. Her world became mine. It catapulted me outside of my prison and into her pages. It was the first book that I had ever read cover-to-cover. Some of the words were foreign to my young mind but I was excited to learn their meaning. With each turn of the page, I wanted to know more about this woman and her fight for survival. I was inspired and once I finished reading that book I wanted more. I had a burning desire to read and escape my own hell through the words written on those pages. My favorite books became autobiographies. Stories of struggling people who survived horrible injustices and still made something of themselves despite the odds that were against them. I went on to read "The Catcher and The Rye" by J.D. Salinger and several "Kitchen Soup" books.

7. BROKEN

My father soon began to take notice in my reading habits and began to take a slow interest in my excitement for reading. Sometimes he would stop and ask me questions about my reading material when he would bring up my food trays. That interest allowed us to start having some small form of communication again. I could tell that his anger was subsiding and when school started, he took the horrendous piss bucket out of my room and allowed me to start using the restroom downstairs like a human again. He changed my bath schedule too, and gave me permission to bathe once every other day instead of once a week. He began inviting me to come down and eat dinner with the "family."

During one of those dinners, he looked at me and said, "Marie, I talked to your school counselor and you're doing good so I think I'll end your punishment in two weeks."

My jaw dropped. I was so excited and before I knew what I was doing, I reached over and hugged him hard. It was the first time we had embraced in months and I could tell he felt a little awkward but he didn't pull away.

"Thank you, Dad!" I grabbed a pen and marked the date on the calendar that hung on the wall in the kitchen. I was beaming with joy knowing that freedom was so close.

That night, my dad was even kind enough to give me back my television privileges. He surprised me by bringing it back into my room and hooking it up for me. For the first time, I started to feel like a real person again.

My happiness was short lived when I was called downstairs for dinner the next night. I sat at the kitchen table to eat and I looked at the calendar to see the word "SIKE" written over the date that I had marked for my approved prison exit. I could not hold it in. I felt my whole body get hot, my face was flushed. I was enraged by her audacity.

"Who wrote that on the calendar?" I pointed.

"I did." Leah admitted, nonchalantly.

"Why would you write that? My dad said I could get off punishment on that day! Why are you trying to keep me locked up?" I yelled.

"Marie, sit down and lower your voice." My dad advised.

"But Dad! Don't you see what she is doing? She likes it like this! She wants you to be mad at me! She is purposely trying to antagonize me to fight with her! She likes that I'm locked away in my room and she has you all to herself!" I yelled as tears of frustration streamed down my cheeks. I realized that she wanted to get rid of me. Her actions were that of a jealous lover as if I somehow threatened her relationship with my father.

"You better tell her to shut the fuck up!" Leah said pointing at me with her fork and giving my dad a death stare.

"Marie, take your food upstairs to your room. I'll be up there to talk to you in a minute." My dad ordered.

"No! That little bitch can get the fuck outta my house and you can go too!" Leah screamed.

"Who the fuck are you calling a bitch?" My dad inquired, sternly.

I went upstairs as I was ordered but I could hear the argument as if it was happening right in front of me.

"You're going to take that little bitches side over mine?" She yelled.

"It's not about sides! She is my kid and you're talking to her like she's an adult!" He yelled back.

"She is a little lying whore, that's what she is! How can you take her side over mine after everything I've done for you?" She screamed.

"Leah! Don't fucking touch me!" I heard my dad yell. I could tell that she was crying and I heard them shuffling around as if they were wrestling. Then the house shook with a loud bang and Leah's cries got louder.

"Get the fuck out my house! I want you and that little bitch out!" She cried.

Minutes later, I heard footsteps and I laid in my bed crying from hearing Leah's real thoughts of me. A woman that had once claimed to love me had betrayed my trust in her. She used me. She preyed on the biggest void in my heart, my desire to have a real mom.

My dad sat on the side of my bed.

"Marie, I'm sorry." He said. I could tell there was a tone of sadness in his voice.

I looked up at him, "I've been trying to tell you that she hates me but you wouldn't listen!" I replied.

"I know. I was blinded by my own anger but that is all about to change. I'm gonna get a job and we're gonna get our own place again." He promised.

"Dad, I can't live here with her anymore!" I reiterated.

"I know. Give me a couple of weeks and I am going to get us out of here. Get some rest, I love you."

He hugged me and went back downstairs. I went to sleep with a smile on my face that night and hope for the future. I thought about the old days when it was just my father and I living together and I hoped that things would go back to the way they were between us before Leah came into our lives.

A week passed and every day I got home from school my dad was locked in their bedroom, sleeping. My hope for our future together, without Leah, started to diminish. Things went back to normal and it was as if nothing had ever happened. I grew angry with my father for his false promises and for continuing to sleep with the enemy. She had made it clear how she felt about me and never once apologized for anything she said or did to me. In fact, it was the opposite. She walked around the house with a smug look on her face as if she knew that she had won.

My mom took my dad to court for custody of me because he refused her visitation rights for months while I was in my homemade prison. Her attempts to call me were met with dial tones. The one phone call I was allowed to make to her, for five minutes, nearly resulted in a WWE brawl in the front yard of our house. I sat in the window crying at the sight of my mother. I wanted so badly for her to save me from my father's wrath and his girlfriend's jealousy. The tides had most definitely turned. I missed my annoying little sisters too. I day dreamed about them all the time. I wondered how they were doing and if they missed me too.

After the first court hearing, my dad came into my room and told me that the judge was going to ask me where I wanted live.

"Before I go into court again to fight for you, I want to know what you're gonna say." He explained.

I paused before giving him my answer. I thought about my life with my father and all the love we shared. I thought about everything that he had taught me up to that point. I thought of the tears that he wiped from my eyes at the hand of my mother. I remembered watching him ride a bicycle to work at four in the morning when there was three feet of snow on the ground. I thought about how he cried in my lap when my grandfather died and our first Thanksgiving together, when he spent two whole days making a huge meal just for us. I thought about how he spent his last bit of extra money to buy me a Walk-Man with the detachable speakers one Christmas and how I cherished it because it was the only Christmas gift he was ever able to buy me with his own money. I thought about how he taught me how to fight and how to pray to God. I remembered all our jokes and laughter we shared all those years and as I prepared to give him an answer, I looked him in the eyes for a moment.

"Dad, you're never gonna leave her, are you?" I questioned, already knowing the answer.

"What?" He asked, avoiding my question.

46

I could tell that he was getting annoyed with me.

Tears filled my eyes.

"I love you but I told you already; I can't live with her."

"Be careful Marie. If you tell me right now that you are going to choose your mother after everything that we have been through together, there is no coming back." He warned.

"What does that mean?" I questioned.

"It means I will completely disappear from your life. You will no longer be my daughter." He replied, sternly.

The thought of living my life without my dad, even temporarily, broke my heart. He was the only person who stood up for me when everyone else turned their backs. He was the one who believed in me and sacrificed for me. Tears that I had held back finally began streaming down my face.

He went on. "She threw you away like garbage! How could you even think about choosing her over me?"

"It's not about you or my mom! It's about HER! She makes my life miserable. She lies on me, she calls me names and you are still with her! How could YOU choose HER over ME?" I questioned.

Tears swelled in his eyes and rolled down his cheeks.

"So, this it? I thought you were smart Marie!"

"Dad!" I implored him but he wasn't listening to me anymore.

"I loved you more than anything in this world. I would die for you." He said through clenched teeth.

"I love you too. Why does this have to be all or nothing?" I wanted to understand.

"Because that's the way it is!" He retorted.

"But... You don't understand." I cried. "I love you, I just can't live like this anymore, Dad."

It seemed like the room stood still as my dad got up and wiped the falling tears from his face.

"I've never been more disappointed in you in my life. After this, I never want to see you again."

He disappeared from my room as I called out to him, "Daddy!" I screamed into my teddy bear. I cried myself to sleep.

The next day, when I returned home from school my bags were packed and sitting by the door. Leah was standing in the dining room.

"Your mom will be here in an hour to pick you up." She said.

She tried to sound sad that I was leaving but after everything that she had done, I could see through her fake faces.

"Where's my dad?" I asked.

"He isn't home. He said that he didn't wanna see you." She explained. "He's not coming home until you're gone."

I refused to cry but her words cut me like a knife because I knew they were true. My dad had once loved me more than anything in the world and that love turned to hate in an instant.

8. Jail Bait

My new life with my mother and two younger sisters was off to a great start. It was everything that I had imagined all those months locked away in my homemade prison. My sisters enjoyed having me around and my mom was loving and attentive, but something was missing. I felt a gaping hole in my heart from the absence of my father's presence. For months, I thought he would come around. He never did. Christmas and my birthday passed by and I did not receive so much as a card in the mail from him. He lived only a few blocks away and with each passing day, my resentment grew.

The happiness with my mother began to sour with time and school was not easy. Despite my best efforts, my grade school reputation followed me into middle school. The kids were more ruthless than ever and I began skipping school just to have some peace. My teachers made sure that my mother was aware that my grades were dropping due to my absences, which only fueled her rage and made her relentless in her efforts to control me. The more effort she put into ensuring that I was punished for my absences and low grades, the more I rebelled against her. She started to wake up and drop me off at school but I would walk in the front door and out the back. When she caught on to what I was doing, I switched my routine. I would actually go to my first period class so that she wouldn't get a phone call from the school and it looked as though I had attended.

I also started to become overly interested in boys and the attention that I started getting because of my voluptuous figure. My popularity with them started to fill the void in my life from the lack of positive attention from either of my parents. I began to seek it out and to depend on it. I became addicted to it like a drug. The attention from both boys and grown men became my personal brand of heroin. I would do almost anything for it. I lied for it. I skipped school for it. I dreamed about it. I stole for it. I fought for it. I endured beatings over it. I risked my health for it. Most of all, I lost my self-respect for it.

My mom's mission in life became how to catch me in a lie. It started out as a way to get me on the right track, but it eventually became a game to her. She stopped seeing me as her daughter and started seeing me as an enemy. I became the reason for all her troubles and she became mine. The abuse became more frequent and intense than ever before. Any little thing set her off.

One evening she interrupted my basketball practice after school because she knew that I had worn an outfit that belonged to her, without her permission. When we got home, she followed me upstairs into the bathroom and began punching me in the back of the head. She sent my sister to get her belt, once she had it she forced me to sit on the toilet seat facing her while she slapped me in the face with the belt buckle. I tried to avoid the hit by putting my hand up that only fueled her rage even more. I tried to hold back tears of pain from my burning skin but my eyes betrayed me. She punched me in the face and proceeded to hit me with the belt repeatedly until my little sister screamed for her to stop. I got up and ran out the bathroom and into my bedroom. She followed me with the belt and continued hitting me and screaming as I dropped to the floor. I balled up into a fetal position and she kicked me in the ribs. She stomped by head with her stiletto boots.

"You lying, manipulative, little Bitch!" She screamed.

"Mom! Stop! Please!" I begged.

"Now you want me to stop! What about when I want you to stop? Stop Lying! Stop Stealing! Stop being a little whore!" With every point, she stomped me.

Vanessa started screaming.

"Mom! Please stop!" She cried.

I couldn't see her face because I was using my arms as a shield to cover my head. She paused for a brief second to catch her breath.

"You're grounded! I don't wanna see your face again, bitch!" She kicked me in the stomach before leaving my room.

I settled there on the floor fighting for my breath, holding my aching ribs. My whole body felt like it was on fire. I knew the damage to my face was severe but I was too scared to get up and look in the mirror. I could taste the salty, blood in my mouth from my busted lips. I touched my swollen face gently as tears streamed, uncontrollably, down my cheeks burning my open wounds.

I slowly got up off the floor and made my way to the bathroom.

I stood there looking at my swollen, bloody face in the mirror. I looked like I went twelve rounds with Ali. My mouth was stiff and my jaw made a cracking sound when I tried to open it wide.

Walking back to my bedroom, my little sister Vanessa was coming up the stairs. She saw my face and looked sad.

"Are you ok?" She whispered in a caring tone. Her words of comfort forced more tears.

"I'll be fine." I lied, somberly. "Thank you."

I disappeared back into my room and shut my door.

***

I began to spend more time at my aunt Camila's house. One afternoon, my grandfather came over with his karaoke machine and they sat in the dining room, singing. I was on the porch, listening, as I watched the younger kids play in the yard.

My uncle Kevin's best friend, Tony, walked up to the house. He didn't speak to me. He rarely ever did. To him, I was non-existent but I had a huge crush on him. He never noticed me; I was just a troubled kid to him based on everything he heard about me from my family. He sat on the porch drinking a beer and talked to Boone. I joined the conversation as much as I could, anything to get him to talk to me. That went on until Boone went inside and we were left alone on the porch. We talked for hours after Boone left and eventually I mustered up enough courage to start flirting with him.

"How old are you?" He asked.

"Old enough." I lied.

"How old is old enough?" He countered, matching my sarcasm.

"Why does it even matter? Age aint nothing but a number."

"You can only be like sixteen. I don't think you can be much older than that." He reasoned.

"Something like that." I lied, happy to hear that he thought I was older.

He shook his head with a smile on his face.

"You're trouble. I gotta stay away from you."

"Why?" I questioned.

"Cuz you're jail bait."

"No, I'm not!" I lied again.

I sat down next to him, on the step below as our conversation deepened. I looked up at the stars in the clear sky and said a silent prayer that he would kiss me.

For me, it was love at first conversation. He wasn't the thug my mother made him seem to be whenever she talked about him and my uncle Kevin.

"Look at me." He demanded.

I looked up at him. He sat there staring into my eyes for a few seconds. He looked around to see if anyone was watching us, then he grabbed my face and kissed me. I had never been kissed that way before, so passionately and intense. It only lasted a few seconds, but it felt like a lifetime.

"I've wanted to do that all day!" He admitted.

"I've wanted you to do that forever." I continued, "I prayed about it right before you kissed me...when I looked up at the stars." I giggled to myself.

Got him!

We were outside on that porch until 3:00 a.m., talking. For the first time, I did not have to pretend to be someone I wasn't. I lied to him about my age but he already knew some things just from his friendship with my uncle Kevin and my aunt Camila.

"It's crazy. All this time, I just thought you were a badass kid. I didn't know you had all this going on." He said, sadly.

"Yeah, they like to point the finger at me and make me out to be this horrible person but I'm just playing the hand I'm dealt." I admitted.

"I had a similar childhood so I understand." He assured me.

We went inside. Sanford and Son was playing on the television in the living room and my little cousin Derrick was sleeping on the sofa. Tony sat on the love seat and I sat down next to him. I put my hand on his leg and he put his hand on mine. I turned to him and kissed his neck. He moaned, which excited me. He turned his face to kiss me again and it made my nipple hard. I could feel my clit pulsate. I straddled him and began kissing him aggressively. My passion was like lava, all built up and ready to overflow on to him.

I could feel his manhood rising in his jean shorts against my wetness. More than anything, I wanted him to be mine forever.

I unbuckled his belt and unzipped his jean shorts. He released his manhood and exposed himself to me. I was nervous but I did my best to conceal it from him. I did not want him to think that I was inexperienced but he had to know the second I attempted to ride him. Despite my complete arousal, he had a difficult time inserting himself inside of me. The deeper he went the more severe the pain in my legs became. I finally sat all the way down on him and muffled my cries of pain in his shoulder.

His moans turned me on and he whispered my name in my ear. I tried not to make a sound but I couldn't help it. He kissed me gently while I slowly bounced up and down on his manhood until he finally reached his climax.

When we were done, he fixed himself and went over to my cousin Derrick to make sure that he was still asleep. Once he was sure that Derrick had not seen anything, he kissed me goodnight.

"I'll talk to you tomorrow, Baby." He left.

We talked on the phone every day, for hours that week; the following weekend I went back to my aunt Camila's. There was a party at nearby hall for one of my cousins that weekend. Everyone was there so I snuck away and went back to my aunt Camila's house and called Tony. He knocked on the back door lightly. The minute I opened it he swooped me up in his arms as if he was as excited to see me, as I was, him.

"Let's go downstairs in the basement in case someone comes." I urged.

He followed me downstairs and shut the basement door behind us. The concrete basement was unfinished and smelled like mold. The light from the windows kept it well-lit during the day. I hopped up on the dryer and sat facing him. He kissed me, slipped his hand under my shirt, and began rubbing my bare, supple breasts with his fingers. My nipples instantly hardened and he lifted my shirt and began to suck and tease them with his teeth. I moaned softly in his ear. I wanted to feel him inside of me. I pulled my pants down and out of one of my pant legs. He unbuckled his belt and pulled his manhood out. I grabbed it and put him inside of me. He thrust forward; it hurt but not as badly as it did the first time. He kissed me passionately with each stroke until I broke free and leaned back. I wanted to watch him inside of me. Each stroke only turned me on more and I began to rub my own breast. His moans of pleasure made me never want him to stop.

"You feel so good!" He panted.

"Please, don't stop!" I begged.

"I'm not!"

My body began to shake and convulse against his. I did not know what was happening. I felt a gush of fluid come out of me. I lost all control of my fingers and my toes curled. I had never felt that sensation before. All the energy that I once had, left my body, yet he kept thrusting into me... Harder.

"You're about to make me cum." He admitted.

I didn't know what I was doing that gave him that feeling but if his feeling was anything like mine, I wanted to give it to him for a lifetime. He moaned in my ear and I could feel his manhood pulsate inside of me as he stopped moving. He held on to my half-naked body and held me against him for several minutes until our breathing became in sync.

I had never had an orgasm before that day. I never knew what it was like to feel that kind of pleasure. When he let me go, he kissed me softly on the lips.

"You're mine, you hear me?" He stated, matter-of-factly.

I blushed, "I hear you."

"I mean it, Marie. From now on, it's you and me!"

"Okay!" I acknowledged. I could not hide my enthusiasm. He was everything I ever wanted, protective, mysterious, funny, respected and mature. I just had to do a good job of hiding our relationship from my family who would never approve of us because of our age difference.

Just then, we heard footsteps upstairs. My aunt Camila's husband came home. I thought we were caught but Tony was quick on his feet. We put our clothes back on in a hurry.

"Go upstairs and I'll climb out this window." He demanded.

"Do you need any help?" I asked.

"No, I got this." He laughed.

As I turned to walk upstairs, he grabbed me and spun me back around to face him. He kissed me and disappeared out the window.

9. Loving Each Other 4 Life

I started sneaking out in the middle of the night and walking from one side of town to the other, three times a week just so I could spend time with him. My mom went to bed by 9:00 p.m. during the week and I was out the door an hour and a half later. I returned every night before she woke up. It became so frequent that he started to leave the door unlocked for me and I would wake him out of his sleep when I got there.

Months passed by and our connection grew stronger every day. We talked about everything and he never judged me. It was something that I had not felt before with anyone. We shared secrets with each other and grew insanely protective of one another. We were both the black sheep of our families and it bonded us. He was extremely opinionated and passionate. There was a sadness within him that he covered by telling jokes and making people laugh. However, he had a reputation for being quick to anger and fighting a lot, much like my uncle Kevin. He was smart and I felt safe with him.

"I wanna tell you something but I'm scared." I admitted.

"Just tell me." He demanded.

"Okay, I'm going to tell you but then I'm going to hang up the phone and go to bed."

"Okay." He waited.

"I love you, Tony." I admitted and I hung up the phone. I couldn't risk feeling rejected by him or pressuring him into saying it back if he didn't mean it.

The phone rang and I picked it up on the first ring.

"You hung up before I could tell that I love you too, Marie."

"You do?" I questioned.

"Yes! I tried so hard not too but I can't help it. I know you are young but I have never met anyone like you in my life. You're so much more than you appear to be." He exclaimed.

"You make me feel safe. I've never felt more protected then when I'm with you."

"You're mine now!" He insisted.

"You mean that?" I asked, awaiting his response.

"Hell yeah!"

My heart was so full. I loved him more than I loved myself.

***

One night, I didn't make it home in time and my mother was wide-awake and sitting in the living room when I returned from one of my nightly trips to see Tony.

"Where have you been?" She asked in a monotone voice.

"I was at a friend's house. I wasn't far Mom." I lied.

I knew better than give her any inclination that I was with Tony.

"Then you better take your ass back there because you won't be coming in and out of my house at all hours of the night like you pay bills in here!" She exclaimed.

"Mom..."

She cut me off mid-sentence.

"Get out Marie!" She yelled.

I turned around, walked back out the door, and started my journey back to Tony's house on the other side of town. I locked the door behind me when I left. I knew he was sleeping and I did not want to wake him but I was out of options.

I banged on the door for twenty minutes until he finally came down and saw me crying on the porch.

"Why are you back here? What happened?" He questioned. I didn't answer.

He came closer to me and saw my tearful eyes.

"What's wrong?" He wiped away a tear that was falling down my cheek.

"My mom kicked me out and I don't have anywhere to go." I admitted.

"Baby girl, look at me." I looked up at him and his warm, dark eyes met mine.

"You always have a place with me." He kissed my forehead and embraced me. "Now, let's go back to bed."

Tony woke me up with a kiss goodbye, before he left for work. It was still dark outside so I went back to sleep. When I woke up the sun was shining bright through the uncovered window in his small bedroom.

After showering and dressing in his baggy sweatpants and t-shirt, I decided to make myself useful to the man that I loved. I wanted to express my gratitude to him, for opening his home to me so I decided to clean the kitchen.

***

"Babe, sit down." Tony demanded.

"What?" I questioned.

"I don't know how to tell you this but..." Tony's face was somber and he took my hands in his. "Your grandmother passed away last night."

"What?" I asked, confused.

"Your Great, Grand mother, Maria. Your Mom's grandma."

I sat there with him and let his words soak in. I was not especially close to my great grandmother, in fact, I only remember meeting her once or twice in my life so I didn't feel anything. I was numb and I felt guilty for it.

"Are you okay?" He questioned.

"I'm okay." We sat on the sofa for an hour listening to music videos while he played in my hair.

"I want you to listen to this." He turned the volume up on the television and stood up.

"Dance with me." He pulled me up to him.

He put his hand on the small of my back and I buried my face in his chest while he held me and we danced. We lost ourselves in the moment as our bodies moved to the rhythm of the music. He gently kissed my forehead.

"This is my song to you. I love you, Marie."

"What is it called?" I asked listening to the beautiful tune.

"Loving Each Other For Life, by Methrone."

Tears of overwhelming joy filled my eyes. Tony pulled back and wiped away my fallen tears.

"I knew you were gonna break down eventually. You always try to be so tough." He said.

"That's not why I'm crying." I admitted.

"Then what is it baby?"

"I don't ever want to lose you."

"Come here." He sat down on the couch and pulled me onto his lap.

"Marie, I'm not going anywhere. You and me are forever. I love you, don't you ever question that." He assured me.

"I love you too, Tony. More than anything in this world." I admitted.

I was living in pure bliss with the man that I loved. We cooked together, watched movies, listened to music and had long, deep conversations about life. Oddly enough, I did not have one accident in the bed we shared. It was everything I had always dreamed that it would be but I had a bad feeling in the pit of my stomach that I just could not shake.

There was an unexpected knock at the door. Tony yelled down the stairs to see who it was. It was my uncle Kevin.

I went into the bedroom and closed the door behind me. Thirty minutes passed and Tony came into the room.

"Baby, he's outside. He wants me to go out with him."

I pouted.

"He lost his grandma the other day, I gotta go." He explained.

"I know." I replied, visibly disappointed.

"Awe. Don't give me that face." He pulled me close to him, "I'm coming home to you baby. We have forever. I love you."

"I love you too, Tony."

I stayed up all night waiting for him to come home. He never showed up. Frustrated and angry, I cried myself to sleep. I was awakened by the sunlight through the window in our bedroom. I turned to reach for him but he wasn't there. My heart dropped to the pit of my stomach and I felt like I was going to be sick. The phone rang.

"You have a collect call from... Tony, an inmate at Cleveland Correctional Center. Will you accept the charges?"

My heart dropped. I kicked the bathroom door because I knew that he was not coming home. He had skipped probation on a previous charge and was facing a minimum year sentence in prison if he was caught.

"Hello!"

"Hey, Baby Girl. Are you okay?" He asked.

"I'm fine. Are YOU okay?" I inquired.

"I'm cool. I just miss you, that's all."

"I miss you too. What happened?" I asked.

"I got into a fight at the club. Looks like I'm not coming home for a while." He said, sadly.

"I know." I said, choking back tears.

"I don't know how much time they're gonna give me and I don't want you to think that I'm expecting you to wait for me." Tony admitted.

"Don't say that to me! This is me and you forever!" I reminded him, "I love you. No matter how much time they give you that is not going to change."

"I love you too. Listen to me though; you are going to have to make things right with your mom and go back home. Okay?"

"I know." I replied, knowing he was right.

"I need you to take care of yourself. Do you hear me? Nobody is ever gonna take care of you, like you!"

"Stop talking like I'm never gonna see you again!" I urged.

"I don't know when I'm gonna see you again but no matter what I want you to know that I love you and I'm sorry that I didn't keep my word about coming home to you." He said, apologetically.

10. Cold Shoulder

"**Y**ou little bitch!" She screamed at me. "How are you out here fucking and you can't even stop peeing in the bed?" She questioned.

She pulled me by my hair onto the floor in the living room. I curled into a ball on the carpet and just prayed for it to be over quickly. She stood over me and kicked me in the back. She was searching for a reaction, something that would tell her that she was causing me pain but I would not give her the satisfaction. I became numb to her fits of rage. Her abuse became an everyday thing. I knew if I could just endure it until she tired herself out that it would be over and I could go about my day. She punched me in the back of the head and I immediately heard a crunching sound. She toppled over in pain. Screaming at the top of her lungs and holding her wrist. I jumped up off the floor to help her but she screamed for me not to touch her. Inside I was smiling, watching her flop around on the floor like a fish out of water but I helped her up. She spewed a thousand cuss words at me and told me that it was my fault.

Her new cast made it difficult for her to hit me with the same power she once had. I was happy about that. Nevertheless, the cast was only a daily reminder to her that I was the enemy and so she pressed on. Everything I did annoyed or disgusted her to the point that even seeing my face made her angry. She was so fed up that I didn't even have to do anything to get her going.

One day, my baby sister, Avery, threw her sippy cup and the milk got on the carpet, I went to grab a towel from the kitchen to clean it up. My mother grabbed the wet towel from my hands and started smacking me in the face with it.

"It's always something with you. You can't do shit right!" She screamed at me. "I fucking hate you! I can't believe you even came from my body! You make me sick! Just get out my house!"

I crawled through the kitchen to the back door and went to grab my shoes.

"No bitch! I bought them shoes. Those are my shoes. You don't get to wear my shoes! Now I said get the fuck out of my house!"

She hit me again in the face again with the wet towel. I pushed the back door open and ran down the stairs in my socks. The cold air hit my body like a thousand knives. The concrete was wet from the melting snow and soaked my socks. I was cold and crying as I walked to a friend's house a nearby.

***

Before long, the new normal changed and I was being beaten and kicked out of the house regularly but because I didn't have any real friends or family to step in, I never really had any place to go. After sleeping outside in the cold with only a coat to keep me warm from the cold winter weather I was forced to go in search of warm places to sleep. One night, the door to the laundry facility in our apartment complex was unlocked. I went inside and laid on the metal folding table to fall asleep. I was thankful for the warmth but embarrassed at what my life had become. Showering did not come easily and I could smell myself. At only thirteen years old, I was hungry, homeless and trying to figure out my next move.

The next morning after I watched my mom leave for work, I knocked on the door to our apartment and Vanessa answered.

"Can I come in and stay here until you get out of school? Mom doesn't get home until five. I'll clean up for you and make it look like I was never here." I begged. I knew I was putting her in a tough position but she let me stay.

I showered and got dressed in clean clothes, even packed a small bag and placed it by the front door in case I needed to make an emergency exit so my sister didn't get in trouble. I ate and played on the internet until Vanessa returned home from school. I thanked her and left before my mom got home.

I walked the streets most days but when I was lucky, I would find someone I knew and try to manipulate my way inside their house to get warm. Most of the people my age were under their parents rule so spending the night was not an option. I quickly learned the lay of the land but when I could not feel my fingers and toes, I became desperate.

After a couple nights in the laundry room, I went there searching for warmth, but the door was locked. I tried to break the lock or pick it but it was of no use. It was so cold that my fingers were burning. I screamed out of frustration. I wanted to cry but I knew that wouldn't do me any good.

Think Marie! Think!

An idea came to me. I knew it was a long shot and I was already so cold but I had to do something. I started walking to the other side of town. The snow was pouring down like rain and I could barely see two feet in front of me. The wind felt like it was hitting my face at a hundred miles per hour and I couldn't feel my toes. What would have taken me 10 minutes in a car took over two hours walking but I made it.

I reached the back door to my grandmother's house and I prayed that it was unlocked.

EURIKA!

My grandma Connie moved from Kentucky and back to Ohio a few years earlier with her husband Boone and my uncle David. She never locked the back door of her apartment despite the fact that she lived in the ghetto. The moment I opened the door I was greeted by warmth and the smell of rotting food. I fumbled over the trash all throughout the floor in the kitchen. It was pitch black and I couldn't see anything.

"Who's there?" My grandma called out from her reclining chair in the living room that she slept in.

"Grandma, it's me, Marie." I whispered.

"Are you okay?" She questioned. "It's 2:00 a.m."

"Yeah Grandma, I'm just tired." I replied as I found my way to the sofa.

I laid on the couch with my jacket still zipped up. I starred at the ceiling until my fingers and toes started to come back to life. I reached inside my coat pocket to feel for my letters from Tony. They were still there, affirmations of his love for me. I felt his presence through those written words; it was the only thing that gave me peace.

I woke up the next day to my grandmother watching television in her favorite chair.

"Good evening, Sleepyhead." She said.

"What time is it?" I asked.

"It's 9:00 p.m." She replied.

I looked outside. It was dark.

"You and your mom fighting again?" She quizzed.

"She kicked me out." I answered, truthfully.

"Well, there is food on the stove if you're hungry."

"Thanks, Grandma." I replied, gratefully.

The cycle continued for months. After our "breaks," my mother would tell me to come home and I would go back to school for a few days and act as if things were okay until something set her off and I was back out on the street again.

Strangers would stop and offer me rides like Jordan, a severely overweight drug dealer that I met on one of my journeys.

We became friends and he looked out for me. He was in his early thirties and he knew I was young but he never asked me my age. He lived in a basement apartment close to my mom's house but from what I could tell, he had money and he seemed to like me a lot so I used him for rides or a place to stay as often as I could. He always tried to touch me but I held him at bay for months. I knew he had reached his end with being used and not getting anything in return. I needed him because he was reliable and whenever my mother kicked me out, I knew I could count on him to come through for me. My life had become a game of survival and I did everything I could to keep my head above water.

One night, I was lying in his bed watching TV when he laid down beside me and began running his hand up my shirt. I moved it. He did it again. I tried to push him away but he grabbed me and pulled me closer to him.

"Stop fighting me and give me this pussy already!"

"Stop it!" I demanded.

He ignored me and continued pulling at my clothes.

I felt like I owed it to him after everything that he had done for me up to that point but I was so unattracted to him that the mere thought of him touching my body made me want to vomit in mouth. He continued rubbing on me and finally I just laid there very still, closed my eyes and let him have his way. Tears streamed down my face as his obese body climbed on top of me and he thrust himself inside of me. Sweat dripped from his body onto mine. I thought I was going to be sick. I counted the seconds until he was done and when he finished he laid his head on my chest. I couldn't even move my arms. I felt so disgusting I just wanted him to get off me so I could breathe and try to go to sleep.

How did this become my life? God! How could you take Tony when you know I need him so much right now? When he rolled over, I got up to shower. As the water hit me, I cried and scrubbed my body so hard that my skin was red and burning.

***

Walking down the street one day on my way to the store, I passed a tattoo parlor and a man stopped me. His dark skin, beautiful smile and charming personality intrigued me. He wasn't creepy like many of the men that approached me. His aura was familiar and I was immediately smitten with him. He gave me his number and asked me to call him.

The next day when I decided to call. He asked me out on a date and I obliged him. That night, I met him in front of the tattoo shop where he worked. I got in his car and the sweet, aroma of his Ralph Lauren Romance cologne invaded my nostrils. I reached over the seat and hugged him, taking in every essence of his strong, masculine, scent.

"Where are we going?" I asked.

"Let's go have a drink."

I was nervous. I lied to him about my age the night before and I, definitely, did not have a valid I.D.

"I lost my I.D." I lied.

He looked at me as if I had shit on my forehead.

"It should be cool." He responded.

We went to a local bar nearby. He ordered a drink and the bartender asked me for my identification.

"I lost it." I lied again.

"Aye, she's with me." He told her.

"Leo, she can't be in here without I.D." The bartender told him.

"Okay, let me finish this drink and we're out." Leo advised her.

We left. I could tell he was upset and maybe even a little embarrassed but he shook it off. We ended up driving around, talking and getting to know each other until he dropped me off in front of my aunt Camila's house. I made sure to look like I had made it safely inside because he waited for me to go in the house before he pulled off. Unfortunately, everyone was asleep at my aunt's house and I was out of options unless I wanted to sleep outside on the porch, so I walked to the nearest pay phone and called Jordan to pick me up.

It didn't take long for Leo to have my nose wide open. He reminded me of Tony a lot, not physically but his larger-than-life personality. He was charismatic, blunt and knew exactly what he wanted. He took me by surprise and although Tony still held the keys to my heart, I began having a craving for Leo that I could not get rid of.

He asked me to meet him at the shop one night after he had taken his last client. When I walked up, the shop look closed. I barely noticed him sitting in an empty chair peering out the window, waiting for me. The street light shined just bright enough into the shop for me to see his shadow. He sat there looking very mysterious. I was nervous and I could feel my pulse racing a little bit. I did not know what he was up too. As I walked closer towards him, he stood up, lifted me off my feet and put me in the empty chair across from where he was sitting.

Instantly, my body began to react to the smell of his cologne.

His sensual aggression turned me on as he unzipped my jeans and pulled my pants down to the floor. I started to panic a little bit but I kept my composure.

"What are you doing? What if someone sees us?" I asked.

"Then let them watch." He said, bravely.

He lifted my shirt and exposed my bare breasts. He took them into his mouth while his hands ran across my nakedness. I moaned with pleasure when he entered me, his long, thick, manhood driving in and out of my tight wetness. Before I even knew what was happening he picked me up like a doll and positioned me on top of him with my legs hanging over the sides of the chair. He bit his lip and moaned loudly as I bounced up and down on him. We climaxed together and it was in that moment that I had lost all touch with reality. I wanted to believe that Leo and I could work but I knew that I had told him a mountain of lies in an effort to conceal my real age from him. If he knew how old I was, he would have never given me a second thought. I was not in his league.

As time progressed, I saw value in him beyond most men and my feelings for him grew. I didn't want to become attached because I knew that at any moment, my lies could unravel and he would walk out of my life for good, but I couldn't help it. He took the time to teach me things from a man's perspective that no other man, including Tony, ever did before. He earned my respect, and eventually, I began to hate lying to him but my options were limited.

I wanted him to love me but he never did. The closer I tried to get to him, the more I pushed him away. My lies were not adding up. I was too available because I was essentially a homeless, teenager with no job, no education and nothing to offer him. I needed him and he did not want to be needed. He was a grown man building his own empire and I was still in middle school. My overgrown body and mature demeanor could only hide the truth for so long.

11. PROBATION

Just before Christmas, I spent the day at the mall. It was not long before I saw a pair of shoes I desperately needed. My own shoes were worn down from walking all over town. I saw an opening and I took it. I acted as if I was trying on the shoes to purchase them but I knew I didn't have any money. I quickly put my shoes in the shoebox and walked out of the store with a fresh new pair of white tennis shoes. I felt a rush of excitement and fear of being caught. I looked around to see if anyone was watching me, waiting to swoop in and bust me but no one was there.

I passed the gift-wrapping tables and asked one of the women for a bag, she politely obliged and I put my heavy jacket inside. It wasn't long before I became bold, going in and out of the department stores with tons of unpaid merchandise. After each store, I would go to the gift-wrap table and have them wrap the items. Several hours later, I looked like Julia Roberts in Pretty Woman, walking through the mall holding so many bags that my hands hurt.

How am I going to get out of here with all these bags? JORDAN!

I found a payphone near the food court and called him. He picked up on the first ring and I was so grateful.

"Who is this?" He asked.

"It's Marie."

Oh, what's up stranger? Long time, no see." He sounded happy to hear from me.

"Nothing much, I'm at the mall. What are you doing?" I quizzed, hoping that he was not on one of his usual trips out of town.

"I'm right down the street from the mall; you want me to come scoop you?" He asked enthusiastically.

"Yeah, I'm in the food court."

"Meet me outside in 5 minutes."

***

We pulled up to the tattoo shop just as Leo's last client was leaving. It was dark outside and I quickly rushed through the door with four large bags. I had not seen him in a couple days and he was not returning my calls. I did not want him to see me with Jordan so I had to work fast and drop off all the gifts I had for him. I did not get the warm welcome I was hoping for; he had a look of disgust on his face and I tried so hard not to let it discourage me but it did.

"Marie, you got to stop doing this." Leo said, shaking his head.

"Doing what?"

"THIS!" He yelled, pointing to the bags I had in my hands for him.

"Don't buy me anything anymore! Don't come to my house!

Don't stop by the shop! Don't call me! You just gotta stop!" He demanded.

I wanted to cry so badly but I held it in. I replaced the pain with anger, as I had gotten so accustomed to doing for so long. My heart shattered but I tried to keep it together.

"I'm sorry. I will not bother you again. Keep the gifts and take care of yourself." I turned to walk away.

"Where are you going?" He demanded to know.

"My ride is waiting for me in the parking lot." I could not turn around to look at him, my body betrayed me again and my eyes swelled with tears.

"Marie!"

"What?" I stopped.

"Please, be careful."

I wanted him to stop me and tell me not to leave but he didn't. I walked out of the shop and just like that, he was gone out of my life and I was alone again.

***

I came up with a plan to get a job using my mom's name and information because I was too young to work full time without consent. I filled out an application using her social security number and birthday. I intended to turn it into the restaurant but I was arrested for shoplifting. I had gotten too bold and my luck wore out.

After spending hours in a holding cell, my mom and my aunt Nicole showed up to pick me up from the police station. I was happy to see her, I missed her but another part of me was so scared of what she was going to do to me when we got home.

In the car, she mostly just laughed at me for stealing and even more so for being caught. That put me at ease a little bit. I even laughed at myself. I was embarrassed.

"Marie, you know you done fucked up now, right? This is serious. You are going to have to go court and sit in front of a judge. They can lock you up." My mother said, trying to scare me. It worked.

The first couple of weeks back home felt good even though I was on probation for shoplifting. I was warm and not hungry like I was when I was on the street. I liked having all my clothes and sleeping in a real bed. I even started going back to school regularly, but with school came a whole other set of issues that I thought were much easier to avoid by not going at all, so my attendance slowly became appearances.

My uncle David was going to the high school just a few blocks away from the middle school that I went too. Sometimes we would skip together and meet up at my house to smoke cigarettes and avoid the constant battles at school. He and I were relatively close in our teenage years. We both had moved on to conceal most of childhood memories together as if it never happened and we built a respect for one another. Probably because I was the only girl that he had ever known who could fight like a boy. A fact that he quickly learned one day picking on me in my aunt Nicole's back yard. I guess he thought I was still the little girl from our days together in Kentucky but I made a believer out him with a few hard punches. From then on, he showed me respect and we looked out for each other.

I eventually missed so much class that I had to enroll in an alternative school just so I would not be held back. On a positive note, it was not as bad as regular school so I went more often. My first week in gym class is when I saw him. I thought I had seen a ghost. I almost wanted to run up to him and wrap my arms around him. I could not stop staring.

"Mr. Aikens, what are we doing today?" One of my fellow classmates asked.

He looked in my direction and saw me staring at him.

"Are you okay, Marie?" He asked.

"Yeah." I replied.

I knew it wasn't him but he looked just like him. They could have been twin-brothers, the similarities were uncanny. Tony was my first love and despite his rejection, I missed him with all my heart. But standing right in front of me was a man that looked just like him.

"I'm done." I said, finishing my sit-ups. I sat on the floor and he stood over me. There it was, that smell. Curve cologne, the same one that Tony used to wear. I just sat there for a moment with my eyes closed breathing him in.

"Marie, are you okay?" He asked.

"I'm fine." I said trying not to make eye contact.

He didn't sound like Tony but he certainly did look and smell just like him. I couldn't help it; from that day on, I looked forward to gym class. I started going to school just to see him every day. I quickly became his favorite student and for me it was an addiction. It was like seeing Tony every day.

Of course, I wrote him and told him about my teacher who looked just like him, he never responded. I kept my love alive strictly through memories, old letters and photos he had drawn me when he first went to prison. It seemed like time was going by so slow and my heart still ached for him no matter how long we went without seeing each other. I was happy to have Mr. Aikens around because, to me, it kept me close to Tony even though he was so far away.

12. CRUSHED

My crush on Mr. Aikens grew and it became noticeable to some of the staff and students in my school. We were alone one afternoon as I helped him clear the balls out of the gymnasium and he started talking to me.

"You gotta stop staying after class, Marie."

"Why? I like it in here. It's quiet, and you're in here." I flirted.

He laughed.

"Mr. Perry pulled me to the side this morning and told me to watch out. Not to be too friendly with you cuz people are starting to take notice."

"I don't want to get you in trouble." I said, honestly.

"Good. So, go to your scheduled class," He commanded.

"Well, give me your number and I won't have a reason to come in here to see you after class every day. We can just talk on the phone like normal people do."

"I can't give you my number." He laughed.

The bell rang and I was thoroughly disappointed. I wrote my telephone number down on a piece of paper, folded it and put it in his shirt pocket.

"You said you can't give me yours. You didn't say anything about me giving you mine." I turned around and walked to my class.

***

I was at home manning the phone in case he called. He didn't. The next day I saw him briefly in passing but we did not bother to stop and speak to one another in the hallway. I stayed in class and did not make my usual detour to the gym. When the bell rang to let us all out of school for the weekend, I walked home alone. Around 9 p.m. that night, the phone rang.

"Hello, May I speak with Marie." A familiar voice asked.

"This is Marie. Who is this?" I asked.

"It's Cole."

"Cole?" I asked, racking my brain trying to figure out who I was talking too.

"Mr. Aikens." He said, sounding a little disappointed.

"OH! Wow, I didn't expect to hear from you." I said, happily.

"I almost hung up right before you answered. I don't know what made me call you." He admitted.

"Well, I'm glad you did."

"I'm not interrupting, am I? What are you doing?" He questioned.

"No! Not at all, I am just sitting here watching television.

Everyone else is asleep." I said truthfully.

"Same here."

We went on to talk about school, the other teachers, other students, his family, and hobbies. I told him about Tony and how much they looked alike. We stayed on the phone until we were both exhausted and agreed to continue the conversation another night.

The next night, around the same time, he called again.

"Can I tell you something?" He asked.

"Yeah, go ahead." I said.

"It's hard as hell to stay away from you. When we're in school I try not to look at you and I find myself staring sometimes." He admitted. I couldn't contain my excitement. I wanted his attention and I was finally getting it.

"Well, I'm glad you finally said something because I've been having that same issue." I confirmed.

"I want to see you so bad. What are you doing right now?" He questioned.

"Just listening to music in my room."

"Can you come out?" He inquired.

"Yeah, where do you live?" I asked.

"I stay right across the street from the school in the blue house with the yellow door, you can't miss it." He said.

"Alright, let me get my shoes on. I'll be there in a minute."

My mom and sisters were asleep. I put on my shoes and left the house.

Finding his house was easy. The porch light was on and it was the only house on the block with a yellow door. It was dark outside but I could see that the yard was perfectly manicured with flowers and freshly cut grass. I nervously walked up and gently knocked on the door. I don't know why, but I expected him to be wearing a collared-shirt and slacks like the ones he wore every day in school but he was wearing a black t-shirt and green, plaid, pajama pants. I was surprised to see him in comfortable clothes. He looked like a regular person for the first time.

"Shhh. We gotta be quiet. Everyone is sleeping." He whispered.

"Who's here?" I asked.

"My mom and my daughters." He explained.

"Do your daughters live with you?"

"Yes."

"Where is their mom?"

"She works nights."

We sat on the porch talking. However, the more he talked about himself, the less intrigued I was. I built him up in my mind because of how closely he resembled the man I loved but he was nothing like Tony. In fact, he was somewhat of a nerd to me and the disappointment began to set it. I was ready to go home.

"It's getting a little chilly out here. Come inside for a minute."

I followed behind him into the house and stood next to the door looking around. The house was clean with a cluttered feel to it. The living room and dining room were connected but a wall hid the kitchen. The sofas and loveseat had a rose pattern all over it facing the large television stand that took up most of the wall. The TV was on but volume was low and the house was well lit. I timidly sat down in the small seat by the door.

"Why you acting all shy now?" He asked.

"I'm not." I defended.

He walked and stood over me, staring, for what felt like forever. I would not look up at him. His invasion of my personal space made me feel uneasy. It was as if he was a totally different person the minute I walked in the door and sat down. He bent down and kissed me on the lips aggressively. I daydreamed about him kissing me before but something did not feel right, it was off. It was not what I had imagined. I wanted to leave but didn't want to seem childish. He pulled back and I was grateful. I tried to think of a good excuse to get out of there. He was standing so close, I felt claustrophobic.

He pulled his penis out. I tried to back away from him but ended up hitting the wall. I had never seen anything so big on a man before; I was scared to death. The width alone was as big as my forearm. *What the fuck is that?*

He grabbed my hair and wrapped it in his hand.

"Put your mouth on it." He said.

Before that moment, I had only ever gone down on one other man, one other time and even then, I was grossed out and nearly threw up on him. He had to talk me through it because I did not know what I was doing, yet there was a man standing in front of me with an elephant trunk and my stomach was turning.

"Wha---"

He put his manhood in my mouth. The acid from my stomach

regurgitating filled my mouth and I thought I was going to be sick. I just wanted it to be over. My mouth got dry immediately; I could barely fit the tip in. He thrust towards my face and I gagged hard nearly losing my lunch again. *If I just do a bad job, he will stop.* However, he didn't. My face and jaws started hurting and I prayed that he would finish and just let me go home. He finally pulled away and I thought it was over. I opened my eyes and to see that he had taken off his black t-shirt and exposed a black wife-beater he must have been wearing underneath. His small arms were toned, as if he worked out often but didn't eat enough.

"Take your pants off." He demanded.

"Why?" I asked.

"Don't act like you don't know why you're here now." His demeanor was completely different. He was aggressive and demanding. I was so intimidated. I wanted to leave but a small part of me thought that he was right. I lusted over him for months. *What's he going to think of me if I just leave now?* I don't know why his opinion was important to me or why I felt like I owed him something that didn't belong to him in the first place. I felt guilty for wanting to leave him standing there with his dick in his hand.

He began unbuttoning my pants. He pulled them down along with my panties and I stood there exposed from the waist down. He turned me around and pushed my head down, bending me over. He inserted himself inside of me. I screamed into my hand while my dry vagina felt like it was being ripped apart.

"Shhh!" He whispered, forcefully.

"Wait! Please stop." I begged, trying to pull away from him.

He snickered and it seemed as though he was enjoying my pain.

86

Please make him stop! He kept thrusting until he got tired. He pulled out and sat in the chair I was leaning against.

"Sit on it." He demanded.

My stomach was cramping so badly I could barely stand. My legs felt like that were going to give out from underneath me. He pulled me on top of him. I tried to sit down slowly on his manhood but he pushed me down hard and I cried out in pain. I could not hide the tears that swelled up in my eyes. My body felt weak and I could barely move. He grabbed my waist and lifted me up and down on top of him until he climaxed.

I got up slowly looking for my pants but I was disoriented. He went to the kitchen for a few minutes and when he returned, I was dressed again and pulled the door open to leave.

"Damn, you was just gonna leave without saying bye?" He chuckled.

"It's late. I gotta get home." I half lied.

"Okay, this is just between you and me." He winked at me.

I nodded and left.

My legs were heavy and suddenly home seemed so far away. It felt like a thousand knives were stabbing me in the stomach. I stumbled over my own two feet and hit the ground. I wanted to quit and just lay there on the cold, concrete sidewalk in hopes that someone would come and rescue me. *What am I going to tell my mom? It's all my fault!* I put myself in that position and I had to deal with the consequences. I willed myself up off the ground and the rest of the way home. *You are almost there!* I cried the whole way.

When I got home, I crawled up the stairs, past my mother's

bedroom, to the bathroom. I pulled my pants and underwear down and sat on the toilet to pee. It burned so bad it made me jump up and that's when I noticed blood trickling down my legs. I turned around to look in the toilet and I froze in fear. I knew that my period was not due for a couple weeks but here there I was, bleeding as if it was the first day. I grabbed a washcloth from the closet, wet it under the sink and put it in between my legs. I cleaned the toilet, went to my bedroom and got fresh clothes; put a pad on and laid down in my bed. I couldn't sleep. The pain left me in a fetal position all night, muffling my cries of the stabbing pain in my abdomen, with a pillow.

13. Pushed Away

Monday morning, I skipped school. I told my mom I was not feeling good. She believed me and let me stay home because I stayed in bed the whole day before only coming out to eat. I couldn't let anyone see me that way, broken and vulnerable. I wanted so badly to tell my mother what happened but I knew I never could.

It took days before my body started to feel normal again. The bleeding and burning stopped and I was back walking normally but school was the last place I wanted to be. I started making appearances again instead of actually showing up. I saw Mr. Aikens in passing a few times but we never spoke or made eye contact again. I acted as if it was all a dream.

My appearances at school took a toll on my already, strained relationship with my mom. After an expected ass whooping, she kicked me out of her house again but this time was different. I was on probation. She called my probation officer and told her that I ran away. I was picked up by the police and sent to the Detention Home for girls. After talking with my mother briefly on the phone, she confirmed that during our court hearing she was going to ask the judge to keep me locked up because I was not welcomed in her house anymore. Without a parent or guardian to take me home, I would have to stay there until they found other placement for me.

I called the only other person that I knew could help me and I prayed that she would. Liz was a foster parent. I went to school with her daughters starting in kindergarten and we were in almost every class together before I went to alternative school. She was an active parent so she was at the school often and always made it a point to reach out to me. I wasn't ever, really close with her daughters but through her invitation, I spent time at their house over the years.

Luckily for me, she answered the phone and without hesitation, she agreed to come to court on my behalf. She was immediately granted temporary custody of me and took me home.

For the first time, I learned what it was like to have a real family. Liz was a stay-at-home mom. Her husband worked a lot but that allowed her to manage all our daily routines. She had four girls in the house all around the same age, including me. They made me feel right at home as if I had been living there my whole life. We had chores assigned to us daily and skipping school was not an option because she was so actively involved in our lives. She knew all our friends and had high expectations each of us. I quickly grew attached to them.

I was thriving from the structure and safety she provided but I was already very damaged. When my mother started to get visitation, I learned that she was not a fan of my new mom. She didn't want to compete for my love and it created a conflict within me. She told me that Liz was only taking me in for the money and she was going to bring me home to her. I loved my mother no matter what and I still wanted her love in return as much I ever did so I took sides, thinking it would win her love. I started to act out and became disrespectful. I began cutting myself and even tried to commit suicide by taking too many pills of my bi-polar medication and drinking weed-killer. Eventually, I succeeded in pushing away the only family that had ever come through for me.

When Liz told me that my probation officer was coming to get me I was excited because I thought I was going back home to my mother and sisters. I was disappointed and hurt when she informed me that my mother still did not want me to return to her home and I was going to another foster care household, hours away.

We pulled up to a huge, green, house on a hill near an old Amish town. Once inside, a middle-aged white woman and her husband greeted us. They had six kids living there and a fully disabled man who couldn't speak. I did not want to stay there but I didn't have a choice in the matter.

Once I was dropped off, their nice attitudes faded quickly. My probation officer wasn't gone thirty minutes before they started threatening me and letting me know who's house I was in. I was not allowed to watch television or call home. I was only allowed to do chores, read the bible and help take care of the disabled man under their care. I felt bad for him because he wasn't able to get out of bed and had no use of his hands. He had to be fed and wore a diaper and a helmet to cover his head. For days, I watched as the "mom" pinched and slapped him for not doing things she instructed. She would let him sit in a soiled diaper for hours and the smell was overwhelming. My gag reflexes kicked in high gear every time I walked passed him.

One night, he was sick and threw up all over himself in the bed. Out of frustration, she slapped him so hard that I finally spoke up.

"Stop hitting him, it's not his fault he's sick!" I yelled.

"I won't tolerate you coming into my home and telling me what to do! You are a child!" She warned.

"What are you going to do? Hit me too?" I asked, sarcastically.

"I will go get my belt." She insisted.

"And Lady, that will be the last time you ever raise your hand to anyone else, ever again!" I warned her.

"Who the hell do you think you are little girl?" She asked.

"Funny, I was just about to ask you the same question."

"I want you out of my house! I'm calling your probation officer tonight." She warned.

"Call her! Please call her and get me the hell out of this nightmare you call a home." I begged.

The next morning I received a call from my probation officer telling me that she was coming to get me. I was so relieved when she showed up. I told her all about my time there and she assured me that she would report the abuse.

I was happy to be back home with Liz and the girls but it was short lived. I lost trust in her for letting them take me away. I thought that if she loved me like she did the other girls she would have never had them remove me from her home. I wanted an unconditional love and loyalty and she failed my tests by giving up on me; I was angry and resentful with her for that. It created a divide between me and the girls and I began to feel out of place there. I was waiting for the other shoe to drop and I would be sent away again. I didn't have to wait long. After missing curfew one night, Liz decided that it was best for her and the other girls, to give up her guardianship over me and I was back in the Detention Home.

14. Cement Walls

During intake with a large female guard, I was told to strip down naked, bend over and cough while she made sure that I did not have any weapons or drugs hidden in or on my body. I was so embarrassed standing there naked holding my ass cheeks open for her to look inside. She gave me a blue jump suit, a pair of white, granny underwear, worn out, blue, matching Skippy's, and a pair of clean socks.

"You're allowed two minutes to shower and make sure you wash your hair." She said seriously.

Once I showered and dressed, she handed me a thin, wool, blanket and the door did a loud popping sound. She opened it and there were a bunch of girls playing cards, some watching television, some reading books but everyone stopped to stare at the new girl. I did not see any familiar faces. I followed behind the guard to my cell. She waived to whoever was behind the dark glass window and there was another loud pop. She opened the door to a small closet sized room made of floor-to-ceiling, cement. Connected to the wall was a metal toilet and sink and a metal slab with a green plastic mat on top of it. A florescent light inside the room stayed on 24 hours a day; the only natural light came from a small vertical window with six-inch, thick, glass.

"They can only keep me in here for ninety days." I told myself.

"Make your bunk. Dinner will be passed out in about an hour." The guard advised as she turned around and closed the door behind her.

I laid on my uncomfortable bunk shivering, but deep in thought. Being there made me wonder if Tony was in a similar place. I wondered what he was doing and if he was okay. I wondered if he missed me as I missed him or if he knew what I was going through just to survive. I wanted to hate him for leaving me but my heart would not allow it. *90 days...*

Once they let me out of my cell and I was able to join the population of girls, eager to grill me about who I was, why I was in there and who I knew, I began to learn the lay of the land.

Everyone was "hard" and new girls were like fresh meat walking into the Lion's den. There were girls from 19 down to 10 years old in there and most of the time they sat around the card table talking about life on the outside of those walls; who they knew, who was sleeping with who, who had a disease, who was having a baby, how many baby daddies they had or how much time they got from the magistrate or judge. None of us really liked each other but we were forced together in a situation we wanted to get out of, with nothing to do but wait.

We were allowed two, thirty minute, visits from our parents, per week, in a small office that fit only two inmates. No phone calls. Our only other source to the outside world was writing letters. We wrote letters twice a week for an hour. During mail days, we hounded the C. Os, trying to see who got mail and from where. Showers were two minutes each and were taken together with a female C.O sitting there, watching. On rare occasions, they allowed us to shave, but it was an earned privilege and the C.O. would be nearly standing over us to make sure we didn't try to take the razor out of the plastic to hurt ourselves or someone else. Most of us looked like we had fur growing on our bodies because it was not an easy privilege to gain. Nighttime was always the loneliest. Some girls tried to avoid that feeling by standing on top of their toilets and talking to their neighbors through the vents.

My ninety days was almost up and I had a court hearing with the Magistrate scheduled. I was so excited about getting out that it was all I could think about. I missed my mom, my sisters and I missed Tony.

I was shackled and handcuffed in the holding cell at the courthouse, waiting to see the Magistrate and my mother. She was in the waiting room and they would not let me see her. My probation officer unlocked the door to the holding cell and came in. I was anxious to get out of those handcuffs and those jailhouse clothes.

"Marie, you're not going home today." She said very matter-of-fact. My heart sank.

"What do you mean I'm not going home? They can only keep me for ninety days!" I questioned in a panic.

"Your mom already spoke with the Magistrate and told her that she does not want you back in her house so there is nowhere for you to go." She said.

"If I can just talk to my mom..." I cried.

"Your mom left already." She had the key to my handcuffs and uncuffed one hand so I could wipe my tears. She cuffed the other one to the bench I was sitting on.

"You're going to go back to the Detention Home and you'll stay there for the full ninety days while I try to find another place for you." She assured me.

"Another place?" I questioned, through tears.

"Yes. We have other facilities that may have openings for you. Just be patient I am going to do what I can." She left me in the holding cell to come to terms with my new fate.

When I arrived back at the Detention Home, after being searched, I was escorted back to my cell. I laid down on my bunk and cried myself to sleep. I did not move for four days. Every time the door popped for breakfast, lunch or dinner, I declined. I wanted to sleep the days away and the times when I could not sleep, I just prayed for death. I was so depressed. *How could she leave me in here? Why does she hate me so much?*

Weeks later, no shackles or handcuffs, dressed in my own clothes, I walked out of the Detention Home and out into the fresh air. My probation officer drove me to my new place of residence, The Davis Home. The Davis Home was a huge, multi-level building that housed kids from all over, for various reasons. The way my probation officer explained it to me, it sounded like I was going to a resort. I quickly learned that it was anything but that. Aside from better quality food, wearing my own clothes and not being locked in a cold cell where the lights never turned off, it was not much different from the Detention

Home. We were not allowed outside and we could only send and receive letters on approved days. Phone calls had to be approved and were a maximum of ten minutes long. I was still surrounded by a group of girls that did nothing but gossip, play cards and argue with each other all the time. We were woken up at 5:30 a.m. every morning, showered and dressed for breakfast and spent the remainder of our time in the Day Room having groups that we were forced to participate in. It was lonely and most of the staff were detached, rude and probably should not have been working for any place dealing with children. However, there was one staff member assigned to my unit that I grew to have a lot of respect for, her name was Ms. Stokes.

Ms. Stokes was a beautiful, older, woman. She had flawless dark skin and long fingernails. Her long hair weave was always in a ponytail or a hat. She told me that she had adult children but by looking at her shape, I couldn't tell that she had ever had any at all. She demanded respect but in return, she was also very respectful to us. She was like the mother of our unit, the one most of us went to when we had problems or needed anything. She was always willing to help if she could.

I was tired of taking medicine that made me sleepy and groggy all the time. It made me feel like I was not in control of my own body. I rapidly started picking up weight and I couldn't stop it. It was as if one day I woke up and added another person to my body.

I wanted to go home but there was no way out and every day I was becoming more and more bitter. I thought that if I had good behavior they would eventually let me go home but my patience was wearing thin.

Ms. Stokes could see that I was becoming more and more

agitated with my situation so sometimes she would sit down and talk with me about Tony. She knew that talking about him and our time together always made me smile. She would just sit, listen, smile and nod.

I still wrote him every chance I could but by then, he was out of prison so I wrote him at home. Before he got out of prison, my mom found out about us and told my probation officer. She had a No Contact Order approved by a Judge so I had to address the letters to someone else. My probation officer had them watching my mail closely. They were even given permission to open and read my mail before it was given to me.

My first birthday locked up in there was the saddest. No visit or even special privileges to call home and no mail came for me. Months had passed by and I had not seen my mom or my sisters and I could not talk to Tony. I felt so left behind. I was forgotten while everyone else moved on with their lives.

A week after my birthday Ms. Stokes was sitting behind her desk and waved me over to her.

"Marie, I have something for you but you can't keep it."

"What is it?" I asked.

"It's a letter from Tony." She smiled. "He didn't forget about you."

"Okay, can I read it?" I asked anxiously. I would have done anything she asked just to read that letter.

"Not right now. After I get everyone upstairs for Lights Out, I'll bring you down so you can read it in private."

I could not contain my excitement. *He didn't forget me!* I was counting the minutes until Lights Out so I could read my letter.

Ms. Stokes, true to her word, brought me downstairs and let me sit and read it.

Hey Baby girl,

I bet you thought I forgot your birthday. I would never forget your special day. It has just been hard getting mail through to you. I never stopped thinking about you for a minute. I love you with all my heart and one day you are going to be my wife. They can only keep us apart for so long but I'm not going anywhere. We are Loving Each Other 4 Life. I can't wait to hold you and know that you are safe cuz I am never letting you go. I love you, Marie.

Love Always Your Man,

Tony

On the second page, he drew a birthday cake and put "HAPPY BIRTHDAY MARIE" in bold lettering. I cried, kissed the letter and placed it back in the envelope. I handed it back to Ms. Stokes.

"Why are you crying? I thought this would make you happy!" She said, obviously disappointed.

"I am just happy that he didn't forget my birthday Ms. Stokes. I miss him so much." I admitted.

"I know you do baby." She hugged me. It was the first time I had felt a warm embrace in so long. I began to sob. She hugged me tighter and pulled back.

"Look at me." She demanded lifting my chin with her hand.

"You are going to get through this. I know it's rough right now and it feels like it's never going to end but the strongest people are given the toughest tasks in life." She wiped my tears.

"Now you go say your prayers. That man loves you girl!" That last sentence brought a smile to my face because I knew it was true. After all the time we were a part, he still loved me.

That letter was enough to get me through a few more months at The Davis Home but as time progressed, I wrote and wrote and never received a response again. My anxiety grew and so did my rage. I was tired of being confined to the same two rooms all day, every day, surrounded by the same faces, the same gossip and petty behavior. The rude staff members, always making threats to send us back to the Detention Home. It got old to me and I was like a ticking time bomb ready to explode at any moment.

I woke up angry one morning because I was still tired, one of the girls I had issues with, purposely, bumped my shoulder as I passed by her in the restroom. I immediately went into defense mode and slammed her against the wall. She put her hand up to swing at me and missed. I followed up with a series of hard blows to her face until the morning staff was able to pull me off her and separate us. It was my first real fight behind those concrete walls and it opened the floodgates for me.

Later that day, I was told that my probation officer was on her way to pick me up. I was excited to see her and even more excited to leave that place.

"Where are we going?" I asked.

"I'm taking you back to the Detention Home." She said.

"What! Why? I wanna go home!" I screamed.

"You can't go home."

I was quiet the entire ride back to the Detention Home. I sat there trying to soak up all the images I could of the outside world to fill in my memory bank.

Back in my cell, where the lights never shut off and neither does your brain, I was waiting to see if my door would pop for visitation. I was so excited when it did. Seeing my mother's familiar face and smelling her perfume made me miss her even more.

Another inmate was sharing the room with us while visiting with her mom. I sat down and stared at my mother, memorizing every detail of her beautiful face while she updated me on her new boyfriend and how my sisters were doing. Right before our time was up; I decided to ask the big question.

"Mom, can I come home now?"

"Marie, I'm sorry, but the answer is no." She said bluntly.

I held in my sobs but tears streamed down my face. My voice was raspy and low but I managed to ask, "Why?"

"Because I won't let you ruin this for me." She said. "He's a good man and I love him. Look, he asked me to marry him." She showed me her engagement ring. "It's a full carat. Isn't it beautiful?"

I nodded.

"We're going to get a new band for it today. This one is kind of plain and it's a little big." She pointed out.

"Times up!" One of the C. Os yelled and the door popped. My mother and I stood up and embraced each other. I did not want to let her go.

Once I was back in my cell, I could not contain the pain. My chest felt heavy and it was hard to breathe. I started kicking and screaming at the top of my lungs. I rolled around on the floor and banged my head against the cement wall. *I cannot stay in here! They are going to keep me in here forever! How could she pick a man over her own child? Why?* Through the vents, I could hear some of the other inmates trying to guess who was crying and others trying to give me an encouraging word to help me calm down. To some degree, they all understood my pain. We were all alone in our cells left to deal with our own demons.

All hope was lost for me after the conversation with my mother and something changed within me that day. I began to turn cold. It was not long before a group of us was discussing ways to escape. I don't know if any of us would have ever acted on it but it gave us hope and something to look forward too. Before any plans could ever be set in motion to make our senseless dreams of escaping, a reality, one of the girls snitched to a C.O. causing the whole facility to be locked down. I heard all the doors pop open but mine. I stood by the door waiting to be let out but nothing happened. Later in the evening, my door popped and one of the C. Os stood in the doorway of my cell.

"Marie, I just want to let you know that you won't be allowed out of your cell for the duration of your time here."

"What! That is bullshit. Why?" I questioned her.

"You were directly named as the mastermind in a plot to escape the facility." She said and closed my cell door.

Forty-six days I sat in that cell with no books to read, unable to write or receive mail, unable to have visitors, no human contact whatsoever other than to drop off and pick up my food trays. I was allowed one shower, once a week, alone.

The time in that small concrete room was grueling. Time seemed to pass so slowly, every minute felt like an hour. Some days I thought I was going to go crazy. I went through a whirlwind of emotions but the one that was the easiest for me to express was anger.

I did my best to busy myself with thoughts of Tony and whenever I wanted to give up, it was thoughts of him that kept me holding on. I pictured our life together without being hidden. The family that we would have and where we would live. I sang songs to him and I went through every memory of us together. I over-analyzed every detail. The hope that I would see him again one day is what ultimately carried me through. I even thought of Leo from time to time. I wondered how he was doing and what his life had become. I was certain he was destined for greatness so I imagined him happily married with beautiful children and a thriving career. I knew that based on all the things he taught me during our brief time together, he was someone that would stay with me forever and I was grateful for the memories.

15. Lincoln Place

On day forty-seven, I was transported to a large facility called Lincoln Place, almost an hour and thirty minutes away from home. It looked completely out of place because it was located in a residential area. There was even a park nearby.

After being admitted, I was escorted to the Day Room to join the other girls being held there. As I looked around, everyone seemed to be doing their own thing. Some were watching television, some coloring, doing each other's hair, playing cards, listening to music and some gossiping. There were around thirty girls crammed together in this one room. Naturally, everyone seemed to have their eyes on me but I was used to it by then.

The facility was different from the Detention Home. They seemed to allow more freedoms but it was dirty and understaffed for the number of girls held there.

After being introduced to one of the staff members, I sat down at one of the empty tables and just listened to the girl chatter in the room. Some girls were curious about me and came to introduce themselves. Others turned their noses up but were loud and wanted to be noticed. *I guess those are the ones who think they run shit around here.* Still, I minded my business. I was not interested in making friends. I knew that the day would come where one of the girls would test me.

With no hope of going home, I had nothing to lose. I knew my fuse was shorter than ever; I no longer feared the system, I accepted it. I survived fifteen years of neglect, abuse, and loneliness. Happiness for me was short lived and I had become accustomed to shattered hope. It became easier to think the worst and have no hope at all.

I made peace with the fact that I was a statistic and forgotten in the system. I knew that there was no way out and I would likely transfer from a children's facility to an adult one, once I turned eighteen.

My third day at Lincoln Place and I was already annoyed with the constant bickering and endless banter. One of the girls came up to me and struck up a conversation about nothing-in-particular. She told me where she was from and why she was there. One of the "I Run This Shit" girls walked over where we were sitting and interrupted our conversation. Normally, I would not have been bothered. However, I was sitting down in the chair and she was standing over me in my personal space, with an accusatory demeanor.

"I don't remember talking to you. Go sit down and mind your own business." I warned.

"Bitch, who the fuck you think you're talking too?" She responded waving her arms around.

At that point, I was already standing up and unfortunately, for her, she was close enough for me to reach out and touch her. I didn't say anything else; I just smacked her hard enough for spit to fly out her mouth as her head turned from my connection with her face.

106

Immediately, the "I Run This Shit" girls were jumping on furniture, yelling and screaming. One staff member grabbed me and another one grabbed her before I could connect again. As I was being pushed out the door, one of the girls hit me in the back of the head.

"What are you doing?" Mrs. Tracy asked.

"She came over to where I was sitting. I told her to mind her own business and she didn't listen." I admitted, nonchalantly.

"You can't do that here. These girls will eat you alive." She warned.

"I can show you better than I can tell you." I laughed.

"You can't beat everybody, somebody is gonna have your number and there is more of them. I'm warning you to chill out, these girls have been here for a while and you just got here" She said, clearly irritated that I had hit one of her favorite girls.

"I don't give a damn how long they've been here or how cliqued up they are." I said honestly.

She just shook her head and told me to follow her upstairs.

I quickly alienated myself from everyone with that one hit. The girls who feared the "I Run This Shit" crew were secretly happy I slapped their leader in the mouth. They were too scared to ever stand up to any of them and the ones who were not victims but just trying to fit in with them, made the most fuss about it. I became a target for anyone trying to make a name for themselves my first few months there.

I made one friend though, Brenda. She was a short white girl with long, curly hair and blue eyes. Her timid nature made her easy prey for them to bully her but she clung to me like a lifeline. I easily grew protective of her because I knew that she was vulnerable to the lurking vultures.

One morning after breakfast, one of the wannabes got into an argument with Brenda and lunged at her. Out of instinct, I pushed the girl out the way so she couldn't hit my friend. That was all the ammunition needed for the IRTS crew. I knew what was happening and my adrenaline kicked in high gear. I hit one of the popular IRTS girls, knocking her to the ground. I jumped on top of her and grabbed her by the hair slamming her face into the floor repeatedly. Suddenly, I was being hit from multiple directions.

"Let her go!" Someone yelled at me.

"I'm not letting shit go! Every time one of y'all hit me, I'm hitting her!" I screamed back.

One of the staff members was trying to pull me off her but she was actually making it worse for the girl. I turned my head and one of the other girls was running towards me, before I could completely move she kicked me in the face. I traded blow after blow with the girl underneath me, slamming her head into the floor for each hit. Finally, with the help of another girl, they were able to pull her from my grip. I got up fast and there was another wanna-be standing there with her hands up ready to go head to head. She swung first and missed. I swung and connected with her jaw. We traded blows for about 45 seconds and she was done. I was tired but not finished, I could have gone a full twelve rounds on sheer rage alone. When I turned around, there was another one. Another wanna-be, trying to get a piece of the action to make a name for herself. She was the one who kicked me when I was down so I went into full gear. I knew the staff had called to the boy's unit for back up. They needed help to stop the fight that they couldn't control so my time was limited and I had something to prove. I hit the girl in the face, she followed up windmill-style and one of them connected, she smiled and looked around to see who was watching as if she accomplished something and wanted everyone to see. I grabbed a hold of her and slammed her head against the wall. I wrapped one of my hands in her hair and began punching her in the face with my free hand right when the male staff showed up and picked me up off the ground.

"Marie! Let her go!" He yelled.

I did what he asked.

"Now what bitch? You hoes jumped me and still couldn't whoop my ass!" I screamed as he carried me out of my unit.

Hours later, I was called into my counselor's office. He seemed horrified by the news of my fight but when he saw me, he seemed pleasantly surprised that I was not hurt.

"Are you okay?" He asked. I could see the concern in his deep blue eyes.

"I'm fine." I confirmed.

"Tell me what happened." He demanded.

"There isn't much to tell. Am I in trouble?" I questioned, trying to get to the point of our meeting.

"No. From this report, you weren't the aggressor you were just protecting yourself and your friend." He confirmed.

He stood up.

"Follow me." He walked me downstairs into a large meeting room. Asana and all her friends were seated around the table with Mrs.

Crofton.

"Marie, have a seat." My counselor demanded as he walked around the table to face us.

"Ladies, what happened this morning is completely unacceptable!" He raised his voice and we all looked surprised, usually he was so timid.

"I want to make it very clear to each of you that this will NOT happen again because we will file charges against you and you will be shipped out of this facility immediately!" He warned. "Do I have your word that this ends here?"

We all nodded in agreement.

"Okay, Mrs. Crofton will escort you back to your unit."

Nearly a year passed in Lincoln Place and I still had no hope of ever being free from the system. During my time there, I ended up with multiple assault charges. I went back and forth, to and from, court. Tony wrote me freely and sent me pictures all the time. He was the only thing that kept me sane when I wanted to give up. I made a name for myself as someone with a short temper and quick reactions. After a while, the "IRTS" crew was dismantled and some of them even tried to become my friends but I never took kindly to bullies or gossipers.

In the Rec Room one evening, the girl that I smacked in the mouth when I first arrived, got into an argument with another girl. She was a beastly looking white girl that stood almost six-foot tall and weighed over two hundred pounds, solid. I was perfectly content with letting it go down however it was going to go down, but when the other girls jumped in and tried to attack her, she came running in my direction to get away from them. She stood behind me and the crowd of girls paused. It must've made the beastly white girl feel like she had protection so she got bold.

"You nigger bitches aren't going to do shit to me!" She screamed.

Before anyone else could make a move, I turned around without hesitation and clothes-lined her to the ground with my forearm. I grabbed the chips I was eating off the table and stood against the wall while they took turns punching and kicking her. She curled into a ball to protect herself. After a few minutes, I broke it up just before the staff walked in. As I was helping her sit down at the table, I explained...

"Don't ever use that word directed at anyone in my presence and expect me to have your back. I don't care who it is!"

Shackled and handcuffed in the back of a transport van for court, I just stared out the window at the cars passing by on the highway. Everything seemed to look different. The air was fresh and crisp, the colors were bright and the sun was shining, its warmth felt good on my skin.

In court, I was not seeing a Magistrate this time but the actual Judge. I was a little intimidated but after all I had been through there was not much else he could do me. Standing in the courtroom, I looked around to find my mother sitting there next to my Children Services caseworker.

"Marie, you just can't seem to stay out of trouble." The Judge continued, "I spoke with your mother and she wants you to come home but I'm looking at your record and I don't see how I can justify sending you home when all you've continued to show this court, is that you are extremely violent." He paused again to look over some paperwork.

"What is Children Service's recommendation?" He asked.

"Your Honor, we recommend that Marie be remanded in State Custody. We fear that she has become increasingly violent and don't think she has learned anything from her time here." I wanted to stand up and slap the shit out of that social worker. She was always rude and pretentious towards me. I could not understand how people like her got jobs working with children when she did not seem to have a compassionate bone in her body. I had only met her a handful of times and each time I liked her less and less.

"Wait a minute! Can I speak Your Honor?" My mom interjected.

"Go ahead." The Judge granted.

"My daughter came in here because she was a runaway not because she was a violent kid. I have been to these places and I have watched Marie change because of her time here. Keeping her here isn't helping her or making her better and I'm sorry that I didn't realize that sooner but this has gone too far and it's time for her to come home to her family." My mom spat.

Tears streamed down my face and I was overcome with emotion. Hearing my mother fight for me in that courtroom was music to my ears. I thought she didn't want me; I thought she had given up on me but there she was trying to right the wrong.

"Does probation agree?" The Judge asked.

"We do, Your Honor." My probation officer stood up, "We think Marie should be released on house arrest, into her mother's custody and be required to do mandatory community service." She sat down and the Judge got quiet like he was thinking about a plan of action. My fate was in his hands.

"Marie, I don't think you are ready to go home so here is what I am going to do. I am going to send you back to Lincoln Place for thirty days." The little hope I had from my mother's speech and my probation officer's endorsement, was shattered.

"If you don't get into one altercation within the next thirty days, I will send you home on the ankle monitor." I knew then that I was right. I was not going home because I could barely get through a day without putting my hands on someone in that place. I hated it there.

One would think that after two and a half years behind a wall, thirty days would be a breeze. It was not! Every minute seemed to feel like a week. One new girl arrived and she was the ultimate test of my will power. I didn't have anything to prove but I genuinely wanted to kick her teeth in. She was always trash talking and testing my limits. Other girls who had been there long enough to know my reputation and had witnessed my anger first hand, tried to warn her to stay away from me but she didn't listen. Under different circumstances, I would have choked her until she begged me to stop but I had something to look forward to for the first time in two and a half years, an end date. Finally, there was a glimmer of light at the end of the relentless tunnel for me.

I had been in there for so long that the staff was all rooting for me to leave, some just to get me out of their hair and others because they genuinely cared and wanted to see me have my freedom. A week and a half there, in the Day Room, I was sitting there talking to one of the girls when J'lena, the new girl, interrupted our conversation and got smart with me. Out of pure frustration, I jumped up and lunged at her. Mrs. Dooley grabbed me before I hit her and forced me to go sit on the other side of the room. I obliged because I knew that if I continued to be that close, there was no way I was going to make it.

J'lena kept talking, egging me on.

"Keep talking shit and I'm gonna say fuck this thirty days, come across this room and whoop your ass!" I yelled.

"Fuck you, Bitch! You aint gonna do shit." She screamed back at me.

I jumped up quickly into a full-on sprint across the room. Mrs. Dooley tackled me to the ground as if she played defense for the Green Bay Packers all her life. She slammed me so hard that it felt like I was hit by a train.

"Come on, Marie! Thirty days!" Mrs. Dooley pleaded with me.

"I'm not going to make it cuz I'm gonna beat the shit out of that girl!" I yelled.

"Yes, you are! If I got to stand next to you for the next thirty days and slam your ass into every wall in this building you are gonna make it!" She threatened.

I laughed and I was happy to have her support.

The next day I was pulled out of class and walked up to the second floor. I had only ever seen it one other time, when I arrived. Standing there, in the doorway, was my probation officer.

"What's going on?" I asked, confused.

"You're going home." She smiled.

"What? I thought I had to wait thirty days."

"Well, I got a call last night from your counselor and he told me that you were having a hard time so I talked to the Judge and got him to release you two weeks early." She admitted.

Thank you, Mrs. Dooley! And just like that... I was *free!*

16. FREEDOM

Freedom was different for me. The way I viewed the world and everything in it had changed. I appreciated the smallest, overlooked things like the way the leaves on the trees move when the wind blew. I was fascinated with the world again and took the time to appreciate it.

The two and a half years that I spent inside those walls had changed me. Becoming acclimated to freedom was not as easy as one would think. I no longer needed permission to use the restroom or raise my hand for a head count every time I left an area. There were no more lines of girls walking through dreary hallways and no more constant bickering or fighting and no more handcuffs or shackles. Somehow, though, I still felt anxious. Always ready for the other shoe to drop. Unable to covet any freedom too closely out of fear that one mistake would land me back behind those walls. I didn't know it then, but I had unknowingly built a prison within myself during my time there. I was hooked up to an ankle monitor just as my probation officer requested but I didn't mind. I was not allowed to go further than our yard without my mother's presence, unless it was to serve my community service hours at a local landscaping company. I was scheduled to be there five days a week for eight hours a day like I was being paid for it.

I knew our contact was forbidden, but I could not get Tony off my mind. I wanted to see him and feel his presence. I felt so close but still so far away. We couldn't write each other anymore because my mother would intercept the mail. He moved and I did not have his new number, I couldn't call him even if I did, because cell phones were just becoming popular and we only had a house phone that my mother monitored like a hawk. There was another way; I just had to plan it out correctly.

Before my community service began, my mother still had to go to work every day and she refused to leave me alone without watchful eyes. She decided it was best if I spent my days at Aunt Camila's house while she went to work. I didn't mind because Camila was not a very watchful eye, although she could be counted upon to give a play-by-play report of anything that she found suspicious to my mother.

Aunt Camila knew Tony pretty well and even after my family found out about our relationship, she still maintained a friendship with him. She didn't like the nine-year age gap between us but somehow, she eventually seemed to understand it. She could always be counted upon to have the latest gossip and she was all too willing to share, especially if she thought it was going to give her a little entertainment. I knew that I could use that to my advantage because she knew the way to reach Tony.

"Have you talked to Tony since you've been home?" She asked, unprovoked.

"No. I don't have his number." I replied trying to sound uninterested. I knew that Aunt Camila could not resist a hot topic.

"Oh, well the last time I saw him he was with some white girl." Her words hit me like a ton of bricks but I could see that she was trying to gauge my reaction so I maintained my composure.

"Good for him. I don't really want anything to do with Tony." I lied.

"Why not? I thought you guys were thick as thieves." She probed, obviously surprised by my reaction.

"Because, when he was locked up I wrote him every chance I got. He stopped responding and then when I was locked up he left me for dead. I can't respect that." I lied again.

"Yeah, that's foul. I would cuss his ass out for that."

"I plan too. If I had his number, I would call him right now and go off on him!"

"I got it! You can go upstairs and call him right now."

She fell for it!

My heart was beating through my chest as I dialed the number Aunt Camila had given me. *What if a girl picks up the phone? What if he doesn't remember me? What if he doesn't want to talk to me?*

All these things went through my head in a matter of seconds; I almost hung up before someone picked up the phone.

"Hello?" I heard a strong male voice come through on the other end of the line.

"Hello? Can I speak with Tony?" I asked in a low tone.

"This is him, who dis?" He questioned.

"Oh, now you don't know who I am?" My palms were sweaty anticipating his answer.

118

He paused for a second.

"I know who this is." I could hear a faint smile in his voice.

"Then who am I?"

"This is my muthafuckin' baby! Marie!" He replied, enthusiastically.

My heart jumped out of my chest listening to his words but I didn't want to sound too excited because I knew my aunt was somewhere close by, lurking.

"How are doing?" I asked.

"I'm great now that I'm hearing your voice. Where are you calling me from?" He questioned.

"I'm home now. I'm at Camila's. She gave me your number."

"You're home? So, when can I see you?" He sounded excited.

"I'm on the ankle monitor so I can't go anywhere without supervision." I said, utterly disappointed. "What about your girlfriend though? She wouldn't be too happy to know that you're around me." I continued to probe.

He laughed.

"What girlfriend? I'm single."

"Oh, you're single now? That's not what Camila told me. She said the last time she saw you, you were with some white girl." I saw my aunt's shadow in the doorway of her bedroom, listening to my end of the conversation.

"Man, that bitch was a jump off. That's everybody's girl, she was fucking my cousin Jamari too." He admitted.

"That's so nasty." I told him, slightly bothered.

We talked for about an hour; I knew I had to find a way to get to him.

To my surprise, my mom asked my grandmother, Connie, to start taking me to serve my community service because she had to be at work so early. She would drop me off at my Aunt Camila's house and my grandma would take me from there, along with her husband who had to be at work around the same time, a block away from where I was working.

When I got in the car with my grandma and Boone, she surprised me with an unexpected stop in front of an unfamiliar, white duplex. She beeped the horn.

"What are we stopping for?" I asked.

"Now Marie, you know Tony and Boone work together."

"Yeah, I know." I replied.

"Well, I pick him up every morning on my way to drop Boone off. I didn't tell your mother because you know how she feels about him so you can't say a word or I'm going to have to stop taking him." She explained.

"Oh, my God! Grandma, are you serious? I promise, I won't say anything!" I assured her with excitement.

There he was, coming down the side steps of the duplex in his work uniform. He looked the same. As he got closer to the car and saw me sitting there, his face lit up like a Christmas tree. He jumped in the backseat and hugged me tight. I did not want to let him go.

"Tony, Claudia asked me to start taking Marie to work and she doesn't know that I pick you up along the way. So, you can't say anything." My grandma reiterated. I could hear her talking but we were both caught in the moment and did not respond.

"Do you hear me?" She asked again.

"Connie, you know you don't have to worry about me saying anything." He assured her.

The car ride was less than five minutes but every second felt like a lifetime. There I was, sitting with the man I loved and longed for, for so long. The only person who did not forget about me, the one who gave me a desire to live when all I wanted was to die. His hand was on my leg and I wanted to kiss him so bad but I knew that was crossing the line with my grandmother so I refrained.

Getting out the car, leaving him moments after seeing his face for the first time was so difficult. My legs felt heavy like ten-ton boulders were holding me there but I managed to open the door to get out. He grabbed my hand as I attempted to exit the back seat. I looked back at him. He mouthed the words that I longed to hear from him for so long, "*I Love You.*"

From that moment on, I looked forward to serving my hours of community service every morning. It was the only time I was able to see him and I looked forward to our five-minute rides together. I needed it more than anything.

My first couple months' home went by quickly and I was doing well. I passed my G.E.D. exam on the first try and even got a letter in the mail from a college newspaper saying that they were interested in publishing an essay I had written. I was still on the ankle monitor and I had a court appointed mentor who I loved spending time with. She seemed truly genuine and although she was from a different background than I was, she treated me like a friend. I respected her, she didn't try to control me or threaten me and I knew that was rare from any adult in my circle.

Tony and I continued to talk every day on the telephone, I had begun calling him when my mom went to sleep. I knew something was off though, I could feel it in my bones. Some nights he would not answer my calls and it took every fiber of self-control in my body not to cut my ankle monitor off and walk to his house to find out what was going on. Those nights, were the most difficult. My idle mind was the devil's playground and I feared losing him again.

One night, I called Tony and he asked to meet me during our lunch break the next day. We worked so close to one another that we each walked half a block to meet in the middle, in a nearby, empty, field. We embraced. He grabbed my face and kissed me for the first time since I had been home. His tender touch was my own piece of heaven on earth.

"I asked you to meet me cuz I needed to see you face to face." He said.

"I'm glad you did." I admitted.

"I don't have long but I wanted to see you to say goodbye. I owe you that much." He said, sadly.

"Goodbye?" I was confused.

"You know I love you and I always will but I can't do this anymore."

My heart dropped into my stomach, but I had learned to control my outside reactions to my inner, emotional, turmoil.

"Please, don't do this." I begged.

"I have too baby. You will always be mine but this sneaking

around is wrong. Maybe when you turn eight-teen we can be together but until then..."

"But, you're all I have!" My body betrayed me as tears spewed from my eyes before I could stop them.

"Please, don't cry!" He wiped the tears from my face and hugged me.

"I love you so much, you have no idea Marie. I can't stand to see you cry."

"If you love me, then don't leave me!" I challenged him through tears.

"This is the right thing to do; you'll see it in time. You're young and you have your whole life ahead of you." He tried to comfort me but I was inconsolable.

"My life isn't a life at all, without you in it."

He hugged me tighter, gently kissed my forehead and let me go.

"I got to go back to work. I love you. Don't you ever forget that! If you need me, I'm only a phone call away. We can be friends; we just can't be anything else right now." He turned and I watched as he walked away. My heart was thoroughly broken. Once I saw him enter the building, I slumped to the ground and cried like a baby.

17. Without Him

"What's wrong with you?" My mom asked. "You've been moping around here like your dog died for a week and I'm getting really tired of it."

"Nothing is wrong with me, Mom." I lied.

"Well, whatever it is, you better figure it out." She warned.

I wanted to know what made him leave me like that. He even found a new ride to work so that we would not see each other in the morning. *What did I do?* He refused to take any of my calls. He simply would not answer the phone or one of his cousins would pick up and tell me he wasn't there but I knew they were lying. He was purposely avoiding me and stomping on my heart.

During the same time, my probation officer requested an evaluation to determine whether I was going to be able to have my ankle monitor removed. She was starting to act differently and her and my mother were at odds. I didn't understand it because I was doing everything I was instructed to do by the court, except for seeing Tony, but no one knew about that except my grandma and her husband... and they weren't telling anyone.

The meeting was held at my mom's house. My probation officer came with one of her colleagues who checked on me periodically during my time on house arrest. My children Services caseworker, and my mentor were all there discussing my progress or what some felt like, was lack thereof.

My probation officer recommended that I be sent back to lock up because she saw that I was leaving a lot during my time on house arrest.

"Well what do you want me to do? I can't leave her here by herself!" My mom yelled. I could tell she was frustrated and just wanted them to leave. "You're not taking her and locking her up again!"

"So, Claudia, you're saying that you think she's abiding by the rules of her house arrest?" My probation officer asked.

"What I'm saying is that we're doing the best we can with the cards we have! She is doing her community service and coming home. This fucking monitor you people have her on is more of a headache for me. I feel like I'm the one on house arrest and I want this shit taken off her and out of my house!"

"I can tell you from my personal experiences with Marie that she seems to be flourishing and doing very well. I agree with Claudia, she should be taken off house arrest." My mentor co-signed.

"Please don't take me back to that place!" I begged. "I've been doing everything my mom asks me too, any time my monitor has gone off its cuz my mom is taking me somewhere."

"So, you haven't left in the middle of the night?" My probation officer seemed dissatisfied with my statement.

"NO! I HAVEN'T!" I said, truthfully.

"Then why does it say that your monitor was out of range last night and 3 other nights this week?" She probed.

"Wait a fucking minute! I know she was not gone last night because she has been moping around this house all week and went to bed before I did and I woke up and checked on her when I went to the bathroom. She was here so I don't give a fuck what that monitor says, it's WRONG!" My mom yelled at her. "None of you motherfuckers have to be here day in and day out with her; she's gotten better. I am so tired of you telling me what I can and cannot do with my own fucking child. I just want you all out of mine and my daughter's life!" She continued.

"I think we're getting off topic here. We are here to discuss Marie's progress and I am in agreement with Claudia. I think she is making strides in the right direction." My caseworker interjected, to my surprise.

"So, you went in and physically saw her sleeping in bed while the monitor said she wasn't?" My probation officer continued to probe my mother. She almost sounded like she was accusing her lying.

"That's what I said!" My mother replied. "That stupid thing goes off when she is sitting right next to it, I've watched it happen and you want to lock her back up because your equipment is malfunctioning. You know what? All you people just get the fuck out of my house!" My mom screamed at them.

"Okay. We're going to leave but I'll let you know of my recommendation to the judge." My probation officer advised.

I was so nervous I felt sick to my stomach. I was happy that my mom was fighting for my freedom but she was so rude to my probation

126

officer that I just knew she was going to recommend that I get locked up again.

Later that week, instead of handcuffs, she removed my ankle monitor and informed my mother and me that she was releasing me from probation. I was euphoric and relieved. I felt like a weight had been lifted from my shoulders.

I tried to reach out to Tony, to let him know that we could be together again. The No Contact Order was lifted and we could start over. He still refused my calls. *Is it all the weight I've gained from the medications I've been on?* I tried desperately to make sense of his abrupt abandonment. I wanted to know how a man who claimed to love me so much could leave me without batting an eye or shedding a tear. *Doesn't he know how bad I am hurting?* I strictly forbade myself from showing weak emotions in front of my mother, which included crying. My endless tears were isolated to my pillow when the house was quiet and dark at night.

That night I took ten Lithobid pills in a half-assed effort to commit suicide. I didn't want to live my life without him, but to my surprise, hours passed before I felt anything. I fell asleep and woke up in the middle of the night just in time to make it to the restroom before violently vomiting all over myself. Afterwards, I stopped taking the pills completely.

My relationship with my mom seemed to be on steady ground and I did not want to rock the boat by telling her that I had tried to commit suicide or that I had stopped taking my bi-polar medication. Instead, I let her think I was continuing my medication as directed, but in reality, I flushed the rest of them down the toilet. After only three weeks, I lost five pants sizes. I was not anywhere near my original size or goal weight but I was happy to see the progress and feel like a normal human being again.

18. Turning Tides

Struggling with my depression and loneliness, I met a man named Grant. He and I worked together when I was fulfilling my community service hours and quickly became friends despite our large age gap. Grant was handsome with firm, cocoa brown skin that blanketed his tall, muscular frame. He had light hazel eyes and long braided hair that made him seem young and hip. He showed interest in me beyond friendship when I first began working there but I was hung up on Tony and barely noticed him.

After Tony broke up with me, Grant and I were paired together for work but our deep conversations while driving seemed to start slowly bringing me back to life. I still missed Tony every day but Grant started to soften the blow. He was overly charismatic and funny. My mom thought so too when I finally had enough courage to open up to her about the possibility of he and I dating, openly.

He wanted to make sure that my mom was supportive of us spending time together outside of work because he was thirteen years my senior. He asked my mother and me to join him for dinner at Red Lobster. To my surprise, it did not take much convincing for me to get my mom to agree.

"So, you're not mad that I want to date a man that much older than me?" I asked her.

"Marie, I've just come to terms that you are well beyond your years and you are probably going to be with someone much older than you. I'm not saying that I am okay with it but I will hear what this man has to say and give him a chance before I totally dismiss the idea."

From the moment we sat in our little booth at the restaurant, my mom completely grilled him.

"You know that Marie is only sixteen, right?" My mother quizzed.

"Yes, she told me how old she was when we first met. I was surprised because she looks and carries herself like a grown woman." He admitted fidgeting in his seat.

"She definitely doesn't look or act her age, that's for sure." My mom confirmed. "What makes you want to date a sixteen-year-old?" She continued.

"Look, I know this probably sounds ridiculous to you but I have really grown to care for her and I want to see where this goes, with your blessing. We've talked about it and if you aren't comfortable with it then it goes no further than this dinner." He assured her.

"The only reason that I am even considering allowing you to spend time with my daughter is because I know her and I know it took a lot of guts for her to tell me the truth about even wanting to date an older man rather than sneaking and doing it behind my back. That shows me that she is growing up and I am trying to think outside the box here because she isn't your average sixteen-year-old." My mother admitted.

"She is special." He said.

"If I give you permission to spend time with her we need to be on the same page. There are rules in my house and I don't care how old she is, as long as she's under my roof, she abides by my rules." She warned.

We both nodded in agreement.

"She has an eleven o'clock curfew, no questions asked! For now, until I am more comfortable, you guys can hang out at the house. If you want to take her out somewhere, I need advanced notice and I want to know where you're going and a phone number to reach you, just in case." She demanded.

We nodded again.

"I can agree to that." Grant said.

I imagine he was nervous although he never said so. The conversation got lighter once the waiter brought out the drinks. His charm and natural wit took over and had my mother spellbound. During dinner, I could not help but think of Tony. *Why is she okay with me seeing Grant but she would never think of letting me see Tony like this?*

I enjoyed spending time with Grant even though most of our time was spent in my mother's house, under her watchful eye. We watched movies, ate dinner and played with my little sisters. My mom would allow us to sit in his car and talk for while every night before he left to go home. When my mother became comfortable with him and we were allowed to go out together, she held him to his word about my curfew and he never missed the mark. Not having to sneak around or hide the fact that we were together was refreshing and a new experience for me. It felt good not having to lie to my mom, for once.

Grant knew all about my time with Tony and how much I loved him but I was beginning to develop feelings for him too. If for no other reason than we were spending a lot of time together. He was introduced to my family and everyone seemed to take to him easily. They had questions, especially my aunt Camila, but he was happy to answer whatever they asked of him.

One night, after returning home from our date to make curfew on time, the phone rang. I quickly picked it up so it wouldn't wake my mom or my sisters.

"Hello?"

"Marie?" There was a familiar deep voice on the other end.

I knew who it was immediately; I just could not believe it.

"Are you there?" He asked.

"Yeah, I'm here." I barely whispered.

"I just called to check on you. How are you doing?"

I wanted to scream in the phone and tell him how he hurt me and that I hated myself for loving him that much. I wanted to hate him for leaving me when he promised that he never would. I wanted to tell him about all the nights I cried myself to sleep because he would not accept my phone calls or how I tried to take my own life because the pain of losing him was just too much to bare. However, I could not say anything; I was just frozen in the moment. I was feeling a million emotions and had no way of showing any of them outwardly. When I finally snapped back, I remained cool and non-chalant as if I had moved on and was living happily without him. Nevertheless, I knew the truth.

132

I knew I was really living a lie to cover up the pain I felt without him and that Grant was just a distraction to numb my broken heart.

"I'm good. How are you?" I asked.

"You know, everything is everything. Are you still doing Community Service?" He asked.

"No. I am off probation now. No more ankle monitor or community service. I even got my G.E.D." I boasted.

"That's great! I am proud of you. So, when are you starting college?"

"Soon, I hope."

"I heard you were dating somebody. Is it serious?" He asked, finally getting to the real point of his phone call.

"I knew Camila couldn't wait to tell you." I laughed.

"So, it's true?" He asked.

"Yes. I'm dating someone." I said, truthfully.

"Is he treating you good? Tell me about him."

"Yeah, we have our issues but nothing major. He's older than you and my mom lets us date so we don't have to hide anything."

"Do you love him?" He quizzed.

"I have feelings for him. I mean, I care about him but I wouldn't call it love." I admitted.

There was dead air for several seconds on the other line.

"Are you still there?" I asked.

"Yeah, I'm still here." He answered. "Marie, I called cuz I know I owe you an apology."

"Apology for what?" I asked.

"I shouldn't have left you like that. I really just thought your life would be easier if I let you go and I was getting flak from Camila and Kevin."

"It's okay. Like you said, now we can be friends." I said flatly.

"Can I ask you a question?" He asked.

"Shoot." I invited.

"Do you miss me?"

"Tony, I miss you every second of every day. So much, that it's overwhelming when I think about it so I try not to, otherwise I can barely make it through the day." I admitted.

"I miss you too. That's why I called. I gotta get up early for work in the morning so I'm going to go to sleep. Can I call you tomorrow?"

"Yeah. My mom goes to bed around ten so call around the same time you did tonight."

"Okay. Goodnight baby girl."

"Good night."

I could not control the butterflies in my stomach or the flood of emotions that rushed through my body like a tidal wave. It was as if he had a personal key to my heart that opened me wide up and shut down every defense I had against him.

The next day I impatiently waited for my mother and sisters to go to bed and like clockwork, the phone rang one time and I quickly answered.

"Hello?"

"It's me." Tony said.

"I knew it was you." I admitted.

"I needed to talk to you all day! I called earlier but your mom picked up the phone so I hung up."

"What's wrong?" I questioned him.

He sounded angry but there was a tone of sadness in his voice.

"I fucked up! I am so sorry baby girl. I should have never left you. I love the fuck out of you Marie. You were meant to be my wife and I let you go. I thought I was doing the right thing but it can't be right if it feels like this." His voice was cracking. He was trying to control his emotions but he would not let me get a word in, as he continued. "That man doesn't even know what he's got! You are so fucking special, Marie. If he ever hurts you, I'll kill him!"

"Where is all this coming from Tony?" I asked.

"Hearing about you being happy with the next man doesn't sit right with me. You are mine! You hear me? That nigga can't love you like I love you! You can call your uncle right now and ask him! I told him flat out, as a man, how I feel about you. I'm tired of hiding this shit!" He insisted.

"I love you too, Tony." I whispered in the phone trying to hide my tears.

"You still love me?" He sounded surprised.

"Of course, I do. You were my first real love. I am going to love you until I die."

"You don't even know how good it feels to hear you say that. I thought I lost you forever this time."

"I'm still here." I assured him.

"So, I want you to call that nigga and tell him it's OVER! You are mine, forever! If he got a problem with it, tell him to come holler at me!" He yelled into the phone.

"I will. He is probably asleep right now but I will talk to him tomorrow. I promise."

"I'm serious baby girl. This is us. Loving each other for life, right?"

"Right. I want to see you." I changed the subject.

"When can you get away? I'll come get you." He said with excitement.

"Tomorrow, around noon. I'll meet you at the library on the west side."

"Okay baby girl, I can't wait to see you!"

"Me either. Goodnight, I love you Tony."

"I love you too, Marie."

19. KNIVES

He pulled up in a red Jeep just as I sat down on the bench outside the library. Seeing his face for the first time in months was hypnotic. My palms were sweaty and my stomach knotted up tight.

The minute I hopped in the car, he grabbed my face and kissed me sending electricity throughout my whole body that made my toes curl.

On our way to his house, he let the windows down and the sun beamed in on us.

R-Kelly blasted through the speakers and he grabbed my hand in his and kissed it softly. It was truly a dream come true.

Seeing the inside of his new apartment made me curious. I remembered some of the furnishings from when we first met but there was a new burgundy, sectional sofa and large screen television in the living room. Vibe Magazines were placed on display on top of the coffee table along with a small ashtray filled with blunt roaches.

He turned on the radio and sat down on the couch.

"Come here." He demanded reaching for me.

I walked over and towered over him. He grabbed my legs

pulling me on top of him. I sat on his lap, facing him with my head on his shoulder while he held onto me. I could feel his heartbeat against my chest and I knew that I was exactly where I was meant to be.

"I've waited too long to hold you like this." He whispered in my ear.

I positioned my hand on his face and turned him to look at me. Tears of relief, tears of pain, and tears of pure joy poured from my eyes, blinding me from seeing his face clearly. He wiped my face with hand and kissed me as if he was waiting his whole life for that moment. The energy between us and longing for one another took over. He pulled my shirt over my head and unsnapped my bra with one hand, still kissing me with authority and intense desire. He laid me down on the sofa and began pulling my pants down. His natural aggression turned me on. He took his clothes off before kneeling down on the carpet and grabbing my legs to pull my body close to him.

He kissed my inner thigh gently and placed his mouth on my clitoris. I moaned loudly as he licked and sucked my delicacy. He held my thighs tightly in place while I stroked my breast softly. He released one of my legs and with his free hand and he used his finger to enter me. My body convulsed as I surrendered to him.

Seemingly satisfied with himself, he stood up facing me. His manhood was rock solid; I put it in my wet mouth with one hand. I let him thrust deep while his hands gingerly pulled my hair. He moaned with pleasure.

"That's it baby girl. It's all yours!" He encouraged.

I could tell he was about to climax but he pulled away and sat back down on the sofa.

"Come here." He demanded.

I sat down slowly on his erect penis forcing my muscles to massage his shaft inside of me. My wetness dripped onto him as he suckled my breasts. I balanced myself by placing both feet on the sofa to give him a better view of our artistic passion. He watched as my body rhythmically moved to the sound of the soft beat playing in the background. He pulled me close entering deeper inside of me and I moaned with satisfaction. Our connected energy drowned out the world surrounding us and we were one in the moment. At the brink of explosion, our bodies moved swiftly into an intensely shared apex.

We both weakened and collapsed into one another. His arms wrapped around my waist while his manhood pulsated inside of me. I felt his seeds pouring out of me as I rested my body atop his. His manhood shrank and vacated my femininity.

"I missed you so much Tony."

"I know baby girl. I'm here now." He kissed my forehead and I moved so he could get up.

***

I tried calling Grant but he wasn't answering his cell phone. I was starting to worry because it was not like him not to take my calls. It had been days since we last spoke. When he finally showed up at my mother's house, unannounced, and without a valid excuse for his whereabouts, it was all the ammunition I needed to break it off with him for good.

I had the love of my life back and I was finally happy. We were not able to go public because of the way my mom felt about him but I knew I only had another year and a half, and then there was nothing she could do to come between us.

I did not tell my mom that Grant and I had broken up. I still needed to be able to use him as an excuse to get out the house periodically, to see Tony and that is exactly what I did. It was not long before I was spending most of my free time with him. He had even gotten bold and started picking me up and dropping me off right in front of my house.

One night, on a stroll through the city, I could tell he had something weighing heavily on his mind. He was silent and I felt disconnected which worried me and insecurity began to set it.

"Can I be honest with you about something?" He asked.

"Yes."

"Sometimes, I miss Briana." His words hit me like a Mack Truck. I struggled to find air and conceal my utter heartbreak but I knew if I was going to get the truth that was the moment to ask the questions that I desperately needed answers too.

"Did you love her?" I asked, unsure if I was ready to hear the real answer.

"Yeah, I did. It was not supposed to be a relationship it kind of just happened. You were gone and she was a warm body. We were just fucking at first then we started spending more time together. I think if you spend enough time with a person you grow to love them." He explained.

I turned to look out the window. I did not want him to see me wiping away the tears that escaped from my broken heart. I gathered enough courage to ask my follow up question.

140

"Do you still love her?" I asked.

"I honestly don't know. I miss the good times we had but I can't get past the fact that she fucked my cousin." He admitted.

How could you love or respect a woman who fucked your cousin while you were together? My pain quickly turned to anger and my mind raced with thoughts. *I loved you every day for four years, I cried over you, I went to war with my own mother over you, I protected you from the system, which cost me time behind those walls and my education. I almost killed myself over you! All so you could fall in love with a hoe? I wonder what she looks like? Is she prettier than I am? Skinnier? Did she fuck him better than I do? If you love her, does that mean that you don't love me? Oh! My! God! HE DOESN'T LOVE ME!*

The mere thought of losing him again made me panic. I tried to remain calm outwardly but inside I was dying a slow death.

He dropped me off at home before midnight. I wanted to get out, slam the door and cause a scene fit for television but I decided against that idea.

"Call me and let me know you got home safe." I told him.

"Okay." He agreed and gave me a generic kiss goodnight.

I waited up for his phone call that never came. I tried to call him all night but he didn't answer.

Maybe he went to sleep. Maybe he's in bed with her?

I fought the urge to call him again and lay awake in my bed suffering with worry. *It's all my fault. I was away too long. But we were doing so good. How could he do this to me? How could he hurt me like this after everything we have been through? What am I going to do without him? My whole identity is this man!*

I plunged my face into the pillow to muffle the sounds of my loud fits rage and pain. I knew I had no control over the situation. He couldn't help how he felt any more than I could.

Days passed before I heard from him again. All my calls went to voicemail and were not returned. Frustration set in. Just when I was about to give up, I called once more and he picked up the phone.

"Hello?"

"Tony!" I yelled into the receiver.

"Hey baby girl, what's up?" He asked as if there was nothing wrong at all.

"What's up? You tell me?" I retorted.

"What do you mean?"

"I mean, you dropped me off and haven't talked to me for days. What the fuck is going on Tony?" I questioned him.

"Nothing baby girl, I just needed a little breather but I'm cool now. We're all good." He exclaimed.

I didn't believe him, I still felt like something was off. It may have been his tone of voice, his sudden need for "breather," or maybe I was just insecure for no reason at all. Either way, I wanted to see him to make sense of things.

"I want to see you. Can you come get me?" I asked.

"I don't have my car."

"Well can I come over? I'll find my own ride." I asked, desperately.

"Yeah, come through."

"Okay, I'm leaving now."

Tony's house was on the other side of town and with no money for a taxi, my options were limited, so I walked. It took me nearly an hour to reach his apartment but when I got there, he seemed genuinely happy to see me. We spent our time in bed making love and everything seemed fine. He got up and turned on the light to use the restroom. While he was gone, I noticed something was different. On the side table next to the bed, written in permanent marker was "Briana loves Tony forever" in unfamiliar handwriting.

She was here! I knew because weeks earlier I had written "Marie & Tony Loving Each Other 4 Life" right next to it and was axed out.

Tony walked back in the room; I was sitting there staring at the wall not saying a word.

"What's wrong babe?" He asked.

I didn't respond. Eventually, I stood up and searched for my clothes that were spread out around the bedroom floor.

"Marie! Talk to me! What is wrong with you? Why are you getting dressed?"

I continued putting on my clothes, but my blood was boiling.

He jumped out of bed naked and grabbed my arm as I attempted to walk out of the bedroom.

"Why are you leaving?" He demanded.

"Ask Briana!" I shouted back at him. "How could you Tony? How could you cheat on me with some whore who's been with half the men in town, including your own cousin?"

"What are you talking about? I never cheated on you." He lied.

"Stop lying, Tony!" I walked over to the end table. "Then what did she do sneak in here while you were at work and write this shit?" I pointed to her writing.

He looked at it and knew he was caught.

"I can explain." He said calmly.

"Explain what? Explain how your dick ended up in her vagina? Explain how I have to go to the clinic to see if you've given me an STD cuz you were fucking a bitch with more bodies on her back then the entire U.S. Military? Or how about you explain why you think it's okay to make me look like a fucking fool for being with you?" My body betrayed me, I didn't want to show weakness but I couldn't contain myself and the swelling tears in my eyes streamed down my face as I realized that my relationship with the man I loved so much was officially coming to an end.

"Please don't cry." He reached for me.

"Don't fucking touch me!" I yelled and swatted his hand away.

"I love you, please don't leave me. I don't know what happened. I just..." He paused. "I fucked up!"

"You don't love me! This whole relationship has been one big joke on me."

"You can't honestly believe that." He said.

"Here's what I believe... I believe I loved you with all my heart and you left me. TWICE! I believe that you begged me to come back to you the last time only to throw me away for a tramp who's proven that she isn't loyal to you. Why, Tony?" Leaning against the wall, I slid to the floor.

"I'm so sorry babe. I never meant to hurt you." He sat on the edge of the bed with his head in his hands.

"You love her and I won't try to compete with that." I whispered.

144

"I don't love her. I love you!" He insisted.

"Don't sit here and lie to me! Just stop it!" I yelled.

"I don't! I have feelings for her but I am not in love with her. Honestly, my ego was bruised and I needed to make it right." He tried to explain my pain away.

He grabbed my arm and pulled me up, wiping my wet face with his free hand. "Look at me! I love you with all my heart. Please don't question that!"

I couldn't speak. I feared my words would turn into wild cries of pain.

"Come here, lay down." He pulled me onto the bed and turned the light off. With my head on his chest, I tried to muffle my cries but my efforts were useless. He kissed my forehead and every time I cried out, he tightened his grip around me until we both fell asleep.

20. Fall Out

"**I**'m taking your sisters to Florida for a week, so you're going to have to find a place to stay." My mother informed me.

"Why can't I just stay here?"

"Cuz you're not about to be in my house for a whole week while I'm not home."

"Okay Mom."

"And I want to know where you're staying." She insisted.

I can tell her I am staying with my cousin Stephanie's house and go stay with Tony for the week. As soon as my mom was down for the night, I called Tony to let him know the good news.

"Babe, my mom is going out of town next week and I need a place to stay. Can I stay with you?" I asked excitedly.

"Yeah, that's cool."

I could not wait to spend an entire week with him. I planned it all out to a science so my mother would never find out that I was staying with Tony.

My cousin Stephanie was my dad's niece so my mom did not

know her mother very well. Stephanie was a year older than I was and her mom did not seem all that interested in the details of her life the way mine did. I envied her for that. I wished my mom was as lax as hers seemed to be.

My mom dropped me off at Stephanie's house before she left to go out of town. Tony picked me up an hour later. It was like old times again. We stayed up late and talked about life, interests, our families, our time locked up and old flames. We listened to music and cracked jokes on one another. While he was at work, I cleaned the house and read books anxiously awaiting his return.

One afternoon, while he was at work, I called the voice mailbox at my house to see if I had messages. Grant called.

"Marie, call me when you get this. I need to talk to you."

I called him back but he was unable to talk because he was at work.

That Saturday, the phone rang and Tony answered it. His face was stone cold, fighting mad, when he handed me the phone. I knew exactly who it was by the look in his eye.

"Hello?" I whispered into the phone.

"Hey, it's Grant. How are you?"

"I'm good. I can't talk right now. Don't call this number again!" I hung up.

I heard banging in the bedroom so I got up off the sofa to see what was going on.

"What are you doing?" I yelled opening the door to find Tony throwing my clothes in a bag.

"Bitch! You got another nigga calling you at my muthafuckin' house! You must be crazy!" He screamed.

"I didn't give him this number, I swear!" I pleaded with him.

"So now I'm just fucking stupid, huh?" He screamed.

He picked up the bag and tried to walk out of the bedroom but I stood in the way.

"Move, Bitch!" He yelled.

"Put my stuff down Tony!"

He dropped the bag and grabbed me by my throat, lifting me onto my tippy toes. I was fighting for air. I could feel my face become flushed. He mashed my head into the wall and let me go. I grabbed a trophy that was sitting on a nearby table and swung it at him. I missed.

"Don't you ever touch me again muthafucker!" I screamed.

"Get your shit and get the fuck out of my house bitch! And tell your uncle if you want too, that nigga can't whoop my ass!" He chuckled.

His friend, Ricky, was there visiting. He came and knocked on the bedroom door.

"Ya'll good?" He hesitantly asked.

"Nah, we not good. This bitch got niggas calling my house looking for her and shit. Get this hoe outta here man!" Tony demanded.

As I gathered my bag and got down to the driveway to leave, he stood at the top of the stairs taunting me, laughing.

"Now I'm going to go and fuck all my hoes and see how you like that, since you wanna be a fucking tramp!"

"Fuck you, Tony! You keep calling me bitches and hoes but you weren't saying that shit when your tongue was in my asshole last night!" I screamed as I got in Ricky's car. Tony was in shock. My comment completely shut him down and I felt justified in my come back.

"Come on man. Ya'll love each other!" Ricky pleaded with us to stop fighting.

He pulled out the driveway and I cried all the way to Stephanie's house.

My visit was unexpected and unwelcome.

"Can I stay here until my mom comes home? Tony just kicked me out and I don't have anywhere else to go?" I asked.

"I'll ask my mom, but she's probably going to say no." Stephanie explained.

"Well can you just ask and if she says no, then just see if it's okay for me to stay the night and I'll figure out some place to go tomorrow?" I begged.

"Okay."

Stephanie went into her mom's room for a few minutes and came back out.

"My mom said you can stay the night, but that's it." She said, sadly.

"Okay. Thank you."

"Let's go to my room."

"Do you have a phone I can use?" I asked.

I called around to see if there was anyone else willing to let me spend the night. I couldn't call my aunt Camila because she and I were not on good terms. I confronted her about being in my business and being all too happy to run and tell Tony about Grant. We got into a huge argument that was a few words away from being an all-out war between us. There was no one else. Tony was all I had and he was gone, probably out somewhere fucking Briana.

The next morning, I woke up and my aunt Valentina was sitting in the living room watching novellas so I decided to try my luck and ask her myself.

"Titi, my mom is out of town and I don't have anywhere else to stay. Can I stay here until she comes home?" I asked, trying not to sound too desperate.

"I'm sorry Sweetie but I already told Stephanie that my answer is no. She is grounded so nobody can stay here." She reiterated.

"Okay." I said, disappointed.

I stayed most of the day there until it was dark and I gathered my bag and left. I went to the only place I could think of, home.

I knew my mom locked all the doors but I checked again anyway. I had nowhere to go; no money, no food and still three days to make it through until my mom returned home. I sat in a lawn chair in the backyard until the wind grew stronger and gave me goose bumps.

The chilly nightfall made me desperate for shelter. I stood up and walked over to the shed. I was in luck because it was unlocked. It was clean but I didn't expect anything less from my mother. She was nearly O.C.D. about keeping a clean house.

I laid on the hard floor of our shed, covered myself with a long sleeve shirt from my bag and fell asleep. I woke up in the middle of the night, shivering. I knew that I had to find better shelter. I needed to get into the house by any means necessary.

The screen on the back door was locked. That was my first

obstacle. Getting it open was not easy either I nearly broke it off the hinges. Once I got that open, I had to figure out a way to get the back door unlocked. I used my I.D. to unlock the bottom lock but the chain was on the door. I had just enough room to put my arm through. I pushed and pushed the bottom part of the door to crawl through. *Viola!* I made it inside.

The door was damaged and would not completely close at the bottom. I was scared and started to second-guess my plan but it was too late. *How can I cover this up? How am I going to get out the house without my mom knowing I was here?*

I decided to stay calm. I checked the house to make sure there weren't any traps. I studied it, knowing that my mom did the same before she left. I wanted to make sure that I left everything exactly where she put it. It was quiet. Almost too quiet. My nerves were completely exposed. *What if my neighbors saw me and they call the police? What choice do I have?*

I sat in silence for several hours, too scared to turn the television on. The phone rang but I didn't answer it. When I thought it was safe, I showered and ate only the food that I knew my mom would not miss or think to count. In my room, I finally decided to turn the television on. I wouldn't let it go above a whisper for fear that someone would come to the door and hear it.

I spent the next three days reflecting on everything Tony said. I knew he was hurt and anger was his way of protecting himself, much like my own reactions, but his words cut me to the core. I tried to remind myself that he was with Briana in an effort to turn my love into hate. I wanted control over my heart. I wanted to stop loving him; I just did not know how to turn it off.

Three days went by quickly and I knew I had to get out of the house before my mom came home and found me there. I rigged the door the best I could and hoped that she wouldn't notice. I locked all the necessary locks and crawled out of my sister's bedroom window with my bag.

I walked around the city for three hours and found a pay phone to call the house and see if my mom was home. Vanessa answered.

"Oh, you guys are home?" I asked.

"Yeah, but mom's mad. She thinks you were in the house."

"How?" I quizzed.

"One of the windows was unlocked." She said.

"Okay, well I'll be home in a minute."

When I walked in the house, my mom was pissed off. I could tell she was about to go into one of her usual FBI interrogations.

"Where have you been while I was gone?" She started.

"I was at Stephanie's house Mom." I half lied.

"Well that's funny because I made sure all the windows and doors were locked before I left and I came home and your sister's bedroom window is unlocked." She insisted.

"I don't know. All I know is that I was at Stephanie's house. You can call and ask her." I hoped she wouldn't call my bluff.

"I'm not calling anyone. She will just lie for you anyway. I know you were in this house Marie. I can't prove it, but I know you were here when I gave you specific instructions not to be in my house while I was gone!" She accused.

"Mom, I wasn't here." I lied.

Without proof, she let the conversation go but I knew her radar was up and she was in full-scale detective mode. *She didn't notice the door. Thank God!*

21. REBIRTH

"Hello?"

"Marie, what's up?"

"Who is this?" I asked, knowing who it was.

"It's Grant."

"Oh, what's up?"

"What happened the last time we spoke?"

"Tony and I got into a huge fight. I haven't seen or talked to him since then." I admitted.

"I wanted to call back because I heard him yelling in the background before you hung up but you asked me not too."

"I'm glad you didn't. It was bad." I admitted.

"Are you okay?" He asked seemingly concerned.

"I'm fine." I lied.

"I want to see you. Can I come by?"

"You know where I live." I replied, sarcastically.

Grant came over and I went to his car so we could talk in

private.

"I'm sorry about how things ended between us. I didn't mean to hurt you." He said.

"Everything happens for a reason, right?" I encouraged.

"I want us to start over."

"Grant, I can't offer you anything more than friendship right now. I am just trying to manage getting over this situation with Tony. I don't have the energy for anything else right now."

"Well can we at least be friends? I'm here for you, you know that."

"We never stopped being friends, I just went on with my life and you went on with yours." I said, unbothered.

***

"Hello?"

The phone was silent on the other end.

"Helloooo?" I sang into the telephone receiver.

CLICK!

Ten minutes later.

"Hello?"

Silence.

"Stop playing on my phone! Who is this?" I demanded.

"Marie, don't hang up." A familiar voice said on the other line. It gave me chills to hear his voice again. I wanted to hang up but I couldn't bring myself to push the receiver button.

"Are you there?" He asked.

"Yes, Tony. I'm here." I managed.

"I owe you an apology and I want you to know that I'm sorry. I was hurt and I just lost it. I should have never put my hands on you or called you out of your name. You're not a bitch or a hoe and I was wrong for calling you that."

"I was telling you the truth." I urged.

"I believe you. I was just so pissed off I wasn't thinking straight. I'll never put my hands on you again." He swore.

"So where do we go from here?" I asked.

"You're still my baby girl." He said and somehow his words gave me new life. I believed that he was genuinely sorry and I forgave him even before he asked for my forgiveness. I waited for his call because I knew in my heart that he would come to his senses and apologize eventually. I refused to be the first one to give in. My ego would not allow it after the way he treated me.

***

Tony picked me up the next day around the corner from my house because my mom was home. He pulled in the parking lot and parked the car. He surprised me when he got out to open my door.

"I got something for you." He said.

"What is it?" I asked, skeptically.

"Open it." He handed me a small red box with gold trimming.

I opened it to find a gold ring inside with the letter "L" on it.

"It's for love." He exclaimed.

I wrapped my arms tightly around his neck.

"I love you Marie. When you look down at that ring I want you to be reminded of that because sometimes I have a really fucked up way of showing it." He admitted.

"Thank you, baby. I love it." I kissed him.

We went on to spend the day together riding around the city, visiting some of his friends. I did not want to go home because I was enjoying my time with him but I knew my mom would be furious with me if I was not in the house by curfew. Even still, I needed to be with him. Our great day had to end with a great night. I went against my better judgment and followed my heart. I stayed with him that night and it was spectacular.

Tony returned me home the next evening and I found my mom standing in the doorway of the kitchen waiting for me.

"I see you decided to grace us with your presence." Sarcasm was her way of life. "I find it funny that you think you're grown and you can just come and go as you please!" Her voice got louder as I stood there unresponsive. I just wanted to shower and change my clothes but I knew that she wouldn't let me. I was wearing a t-shirt and sweat pants that Tony gave me to change into the night before.

"See, I did a little research of my own because I knew you were hiding something from me and as it turns out you were hiding a whole lot!" She yelled.

"You haven't been staying at your cousin's house you've been laid up with that son-of-bitch, Tony, this whole fucking time! Lying to my face!" She threw my diary on the floor in front of me.

"You read my diary?" I asked, trying to conceal my agitation.

"You're damn right, I did!" She boasted.

I stood there, trying to remember everything that I had written. I knew all my secrets were there and now she knew everything.

"You don't have anything to say?"

"What can I say Mom? You read it all." I said with a hint of sarcasm in my tone.

"Bitch, you better watch your mouth when you're talking to me. I am not one of these little girls on the street. I'm your fucking mother and you will show me some goddamn respect in my own house!"

She walked closer towards me and raised her hand to smack me but I blocked her from hitting my face, which only further enraged her.

"Get the fuck out of my house you little tramp! NOW!" She screamed in my face. I turned towards my bedroom to get my things.

"No!" She grabbed my arm. "Where the fuck do you think you're going?"

"You just told me to get out. I'm getting my stuff."

She laughed.

"Everything in this house belongs to me. You don't have anything to get. Those clothes are mine now." She exclaimed.

"Mom, you didn't pay for my clothes." I reminded her.

"I don't give a fuck who paid for them. They're in my house so they belong to me!"

"What am I supposed to do with nothing to wear?" I asked.

"That isn't my concern. You think you're grown so figure it the fuck out!"

"Mom, just let me get some of my clothes and I'll leave." I said calmly.

"Oh, you're going to leave. If I have to call the police to have them escort your ass outta here you will be leaving my house today!"

I wanted to hold my ground and demand that she give me my things but I knew that would make the situation worse. I walked over to the front door and pleaded with her one more time.

"Mom, please?" I asked.

"Get the fuck out!"

"Fine!" I yelled back at her. "All you're going to do is kick me out and call the police again and lie! You'll tell them that I ran away to get me locked up again! That is your M.O. right, Mom?" I no longer feared the system or my mother's wrath. I wanted to have a good relationship with her but not if it cost me my relationship with Tony.

I saw it coming and I turned to try to dodge it but I wasn't quick enough, she threw a full can of Sierra Mist into my back that felt a speeding bullet. It nearly buckled me; she ran towards me and started hitting me in the back of my head with powerful blows from her heavy fists. I pushed the screen door open and ran in my backless white Skippy's down the street.

I reached a payphone nearby and searched for change in my purse. I had $138.36 to my name. I used my last little bit of change to call Tony to see if he would come and get me. *No answer.*

It was getting late and the sun was going down. I started my journey and I passed my aunt Camila's house on the way. My cousins were sitting outside on the porch. I stopped to speak and my aunt came outside.

"What are you doing here? Get out of my yard!" She yelled.

"I didn't come to see you. Take your nosey ass back in the

house!" I yelled back.

"You're at my house bitch, I don't care who you're here to see!"

"Bitch?" I tried to run up the porch steps but my cousin stopped me.

"Come on, Cuz! Just go." He pleaded with me using all his strength to hold me back.

"That's right! Get the fuck away from my house before I call the cops." She screamed.

"You're lucky he's here and your scary ass won't come off the porch." I just turned and started walking away.

It was a lonely walk to Tony's house. I prayed that he was home and more than that, I prayed that he was alone.

When I reached his apartment, I could see his bedroom light was on and as I got closer to the door, I could hear the music playing. I banged on the door but no one answered. *Please God, do not let Briana be here!* I knocked for fifteen minutes and gave up. I sat on the steps by the door and an overwhelming sense of defeat came over me. My anger towards my mother and my aunt turned to sadness. Tony was all I had left. I knew he was home but he was not answering the door. I gathered up enough courage out of my own desperation to run down the stairs, pick up a rock and throw it at his bedroom window. The first one did nothing. The second one hit hard and I thought I cracked the window. He popped up trying to see who was there. When he saw it was me, a look of disappointment etched across his face and I sat on the steps waiting for him to open the door.

"What are you doing here?" He asked confused and seemingly annoyed.

160

"My mom kicked me out." I admitted.

"Come in." He said with chagrin.

I followed behind him into his dark apartment and sat down on the sectional sofa; he went into the bedroom.

His indifferent demeanor only added to my sadness. I felt like I was burdening him by being there and I began to cry uncontrollably.

"Marie!" He yelled my name from the other room. "Come here!"

I couldn't move. *How did my life end up this way?*

I thought he had gone to sleep because it seemed like ten minutes passed and there I was, still sitting on the couch sobbing with no end in sight.

He appeared in the doorway of the dark living room.

"Please stop crying and tell me what happened."

"She. Found. Out. About. Us." I cried, barely about to get out a full sentence from lack of air. "She. Threw. A. Full. Can. Of. Pop. At. Me!"

Tony walked over and sat next to me. He put his arms around me and held me tight. His embrace calmed my sobs but my tears flowed freely.

"Listen to me." He lifted my face to look at him, and with the small light coming in through the window, I could see his face.

"You're not going back there ever again! Do you hear me?" He asked. "She wouldn't let me get my clothes." I told him.

"Fuck them clothes! I do not ever want you to have to ask anyone of them for shit! If you need something, you come to me! Do you understand?" I nodded in agreement.

"Come to bed. It's late and I have to work in the morning."

Tony grabbed my hand and walked me into his room. He held me tight against his bare chest as I silently cried myself to sleep.

22. Through Fire

For days, I wore Tony's baggy clothes. I washed my undergarments in the sink and hung them to dry until he was paid. He took me to Wal-Mart and bought me a few outfits, new shoes and underwear. I begged him to let me call my mom and ask her for my things so he didn't have to spend the money that he would have used to pay the gas bill, on my new wardrobe. He refused and I felt guilty because we were stuck taking cold showers.

Money was tight and he complained because he was trying to stay out the streets and go legit but he was only making pennies compared to what he was used to making when he was hustling. There was not much food in the house because he needed to keep a roof over our heads.

Out of desperation, we went grocery shopping for few weeks' worth of groceries and paid for it with a post-dated check. Luckily, the cashier didn't notice the date on the check because his bank account was nearly in the negative. The struggle seemed to bring us closer together as a team. Giving up on each other was not an option. It was us against the world. Something had to give, eventually.

Finally, while he was at work, I reached out and called to check on my sisters.

"How are you guys doing?" I asked Vanessa.

"We're doing good."

"Did Mom ever call the police on me?"

"I don't think so. She's home and she said to give her the phone she wants to talk to you." Vanessa explained. I almost hung up but I wanted to hear what she had to say.

"Marie, I want to take you to lunch this weekend." My mother said.

"Uhh..."

"I didn't call the police on you so it's not some kind of ambush, I just want to talk to you." She explained.

"Okay."

"I'll pick you up at your grandma's house on Saturday."

"Okay."

When Tony got home that evening, I told him that I called my sister and spoke with my mom. He was not happy about it but he didn't want my mother and I at odds any more than I wanted to be. He was worried that she might have some plan to get me locked up again, but he took her at her word and encouraged me to go and talk to her.

Saturday afternoon my mom picked me up from my grandmother's house and we went to Bob Evan's to eat and talk with both my sisters. I was glad to see them I missed them a lot. Despite everything going on in my life, my love for those girls was paramount.

"Where have you been staying?" My mother probed.

"Here and there." I lied.

"You don't have to lie to me. I know you've been staying with Tony, I know where he lives." She admitted.

A rush of fear came over me and I must have looked as if I had seen a ghost.

"Oh, relax!" She laughed. "If I wanted to send the police to come get you, I would've done it by now."

"Why haven't you?" I asked curiously.

"What good is that going to do? Apparently, you guys are hell bent on being together. Although, I cannot understand what you see in him. You're safe... For now."

I was happy to hear that she was okay with my living arrangements but there was a warning undertone in her voice that made it feel like the other shoe was going to drop and I just didn't know when.

"I get it. You love him and you are obviously willing to sacrifice your whole life and everyone in it for that man. I brought you here to tell you that I am taking your sisters and moving to Florida."

My heart sunk. *Is she going to try to take me with her? I'll never go!*

"When?" I asked.

"In three weeks. I already have a job and we're going to stay with your uncle until I find a place." She explained.

"So, what about me?" I asked, holding my breath.

"Honestly Marie, I don't want to take you with me. My life is great when you are not around for me to worry about but you are still my daughter and I have a responsibility to take care of you until you are eighteen. I have to decide whether to take you with me and be miserable or leave you here where there's no one to really watch over you except your grandma and we both know how good she does that." She said sarcastically.

Hearing her admit how miserable I made her life and not wanting to take me with her was like a knife to my heart but my body would not react.

"I'll be fine, Mom." I lied, fearful of her absence in my life for the first time since I was a small child. I turned to look at Vanessa.

"Are you excited about moving to Florida?" I asked with fake enthusiasm.

"Not really!" She said uninterested in the adventure before her.

"I gotta go to the bathroom. I'll be right back."

I sat in the stall of the bathroom listening to other patrons come and go as I shed my tears. Beyond my mother's harsh truth, my sisters were being taken from me and I didn't know if or when I would ever see them again. My heart was bleeding with pain.

Come on Marie! Pull it together! Fix your face!

I cleaned my face in the mirror trying to conceal my pain. My eyes were still red. *Don't look at her!*

She dropped me off at my grandma's house and handed me a few bags of clothes. I hugged my sisters' goodbye. I didn't know if it would be the last time.

"Bye, Mom." I waved at her.

"Bye, Marie."

At home, I tried to hold it together and put on my tough façade but Tony saw right through me.

"I know you feel like they're leaving you and you're gonna be left alone." He pushed.

"What are you talking about?" I questioned.

"I know you! That tough shit only works on people that don't know your heart and I know that it's hurting you."

"Of course, it is but I'm used to it by now."

"You'll never get used to being hurt by people that you love." He explained.

"I just don't want to feel anything anymore." I admitted.

"Don't say that. Your heart is pure and you love unconditionally, no matter how many times you're hurt. That is what makes you so beautiful."

"I'm just tired of being left behind and forgotten by people that are supposed to love me." I replied.

"I know. But I'm here and I'll never leave you, no matter what!"

23. POISON

We drove to meet one of Tony's friends at a nearby gas station. Money had gotten so tight that he decided to hit the streets one last time just to get our heads above water. He was meeting his friend to make the purchase and I insisted on going with him, he allowed me to tag along to avoid an argument.

He hopped in the other car and I waited for him. It only took a few minutes and we were back on our way home. Once we got there, Tony pulled out a red, porcelain plate from the cupboard and placed the contents of a baggy on top of it.

A large, milky, white rock. I reached for it and he slapped my hand.

"Don't touch this shit, its poison! It will get in your system just from handling it without gloves." He warned.

"So where are your gloves?" I asked with my hand on my hip.

"I'm used to touching this shit but don't let me see you touching it. EVER!"

"Okay!" I conceded.

I watched as he used a razor blade to cut the rock down into small pieces and placed them back into the original bag.

"Shouldn't you be putting them in separate baggies?" I asked, naively.

"If the police catch you and you have a bunch of bags, you're automatically getting charged with distribution. If they catch you with one bag, you can get away with saying it's for personal use and that's a lesser charge."

Times were looking up for us. We had money in our pockets because it was payday, full bellies and soon we would have enough money to get the gas turned back on. There was hope at the end of our struggle.

We got in the Jeep to catch a sale. He did not want me to go but again, I made a fuss about not being left at home alone. Really, I still did not trust him. I was scared that he might be out having fun and somehow realize that I was weighing him down, so he obliged my insecurity.

We drove the back way to the other side of town, passing the police station. It was after midnight and there were no stores nearby, only houses with porch lights on. Suddenly, the Jeep started slowing down and Tony looked scared.

"What's wrong?" I asked nervously.

"We forgot to put gas in the car!" He yelled, hitting the steering wheel out of frustration.

We sat there for several seconds on the side of the road thinking of what to do next. He decided that we should get out and walk to the gas station to ask for help, but in either direction, the gas station was miles away.

Before we were able to get out of the car, red and blue lights shined brightly in the rearview mirror.

"FUCK!" He yelled.

My heart raced.

"What are we gonna do?" I asked.

"Just be cool."

"What seems to be the trouble?" The officer asked as he approached the Jeep.

"We just ran out of gas, that's all." Tony explained.

"Can I see your license, registration and insurance?"

"I don't have my license on me but here is my registration and insurance card, Officer."

"Why don't you have your license?" The officer asked.

"I left my wallet at home." He lied, knowing the car was not registered in his name and his license was suspended.

The officer wrote his name and information down on a small notepad and walked back to his car. Minutes later, another police car pulled up behind him.

I opened the passenger side door and both officers yelled at me to shut it as they all rushed my side of the car. Tony saw an opening and he took it. He jumped out in jean shorts, untied Timberland boots, and ran into the darkness.

"Tony, NO!" I yelled. Scared of what they would do to him if he were caught.

The officer asked me to step out of the car and searched my purse. I silently prayed that they wouldn't catch him.

"Oh, we're going to catch him and he's going to jail for a while. You can be certain about that!" The officer insisted as if he was reading my thoughts.

"Please, just don't hurt him!" I begged.

"Well, he shouldn't have run. Just have a seat." He opened the back door to his cruiser and I got in.

After hearing a bunch of noise on the radio for several minutes, two cops got into the car and started driving back to the police station.

"Did they catch him?" I asked anxiously.

"Not yet, but they will." He said, certain of himself.

At the police station, I was escorted into an office where I was told to call my parents.

"My mom lives in Florida. I live with my grandma." I lied.

I dialed her number and prayed that she would pick up the phone so I did not have to sit overnight in a cold jail cell.

"Hello?" She answered.

"Grandma! I need your help."

"Marie?"

"You told me I could call you if I ever needed anything and I need you right now!"

"What's wrong?"

"I'm at the police station and I need you to come pick me up right now or they're going to take me to jail."

"What happened?"

"I'll tell you when you get here but whatever you do, please don't call my mom!" I begged.

"I'll be there in a little bit." She said with disappointment.

Boone was waiting for us in the car when we walked out of the police station. He listened quietly as I told my grandma what happened.

"Please don't tell my mom!" I begged.

"Marie, I have to tell your mom. If she finds out from someone else that I knew..."

"Well, let me tell her!"

"Okay, I'll give you a couple days to tell her but if you don't, I will!" She warned me.

"Thank you so much, Grandma."

She dropped me off in front of the apartment I shared with Tony and I ran up the stairs and locked the door behind me. The house was quiet. Too quiet. I turned the radio on to drown out the sound of my screams from the neighbors.

What am I going to do now? God, why did you let this happen? I cannot live without him again! I sobbed so hard I could taste the salty snot running from my nose. I went to the kitchen to get some water and before I could fill the glass, I fell to the floor unable to breathe as if all the air was suddenly sucked out of the room.

I was once again in a situation that I had no control over. I could not help the one person who I would gladly give my life for.

Suddenly, there was a loud banging on the door. It scared me out of my stupor.

"Baby, it's me! Open the door!"

I got up and ran to the door. The minute I opened it, he fell into my arms. He was soaking wet from head to toe but I didn't care. He grabbed my face and wiped my tears.

"I've never been so fucking happy to see your face!" He exclaimed.

"Me either!"

"Why are you crying?" He said through panted breath.

"Because I thought I'd lost you again."

"Hell no! Those muthafuckas couldn't catch me!" He laughed.

"What happened?"

"I was running to get away from you with that shit I had on me. I ran and jumped a fence into someone's backyard. There was one cop who was right on my ass the whole time and I thought I was gonna be caught so I dropped it in a puddle of water. I got to the highway and I tripped in the middle of the road. He was like, 'I got your ass now,' but I hopped up quick and got across. I hid behind some bushes next to the gas station until this old white man and his son came riding by and asked me if I needed help. I hid in the backseat and they drove me all the way home. I offered him some money but he wouldn't even take it. I thought I was gonna have to break in because I left my keys in the car but I knew someone was here when I saw the bottom door was unlocked." Tony explained.

I wrapped my arms around his neck and didn't want to let him go.

"I told you baby! I'll never leave you!" He kissed my forehead.

After showering and changing his clothes, he couldn't sleep. He laid awake in the bed and I fell asleep on his chest.

I woke up to an empty bed and voices in the living room. His cousin Jamari was there.

"If I don't miss any work, in two weeks I get a thousand-dollar bonus. That is gonna get us through." Tony said.

I got up and went to join them in the living room.

"What time is it?" I asked.

"Almost noon." Tony answered.

There was a knock at the door and everyone froze.

"Marie, I know you're in there!" I heard my mom's voice.

FUCK!

I peeked through the curtain and my mom was standing there with her fiancé and my grandmother.

"Get your shit and let's go!" She yelled.

I turned to Tony with fear etched across my face.

"Babe, I got to go or she's going to call the cops. I'll be back okay?" I assured him.

"I know. I love you!" He kissed me.

I put my shoes on, left all my stuff and walked out the door.

Tony and Jamari followed behind me and stood at the top of the steps. They watched as I got into my mom's, fiancé's car.

"I love you! I'll be back!" I yelled to him.

"No, the fuck you won't! Get your ass in the car!" My mom yelled at me.

"You should be ashamed of yourself! They should've locked your ass up!" My mom screamed at Tony.

"They should lock your ass up right along with me!" Tony antagonized.

"Don't listen to her!" I screamed.

174

"Shut the fuck up you little bitch!" My mom yelled as she backed out of the driveway.

"You shut the fuck up!" I yelled back, boldly.

She was pulling her car out of the driveway; I turned to see her come to a complete stop. She jumped out and rushed towards the car I was in. My window was down and I knew if I did not get out the car, she was going to use the open window as an advantage and I would be defenseless. I got out of the car just in time.

She swung and hit me in the face. Her large diamond ring cut my nose causing it to bleed. I tried to back away from her but she kept inching towards me and she swung again. I wish I could say that I was able to hold my composure and walk away. I can't. The minute I saw the blood all my repressed rage surfaced. I did not see my mother anymore. My anger took over and I began to fight her as if she was one of the girls behind those concrete walls. With every blow, I felt vindicated, sixteen years of abuse and neglect poured out of me like a water faucet. Her fiancé and my grandmother tried to separate us but I was an avalanche of raw emotion that could not be stopped. It was not until I looked into my mother's beautiful eyes and saw the pain that I was causing her that I finally withdrew.

Somehow, hurting her did not make me feel better. In spite of all that had happened between us, she was still my mother and I did not know how to stop loving her. I wanted to hug her and tell her that I was sorry. I didn't want to hurt her but the days of allowing her to put her hands on me were long gone. Before I could say anything, she yelled, "Call the police!" and I ran. In backless Skippy's, out of shape and out of breath, I ran across the busy street behind our apartment into a nearby church parking lot. I tried every door to look for a place to hide but they were locked. I heard a car behind me and I knew I was caught. Suddenly an unfamiliar, tan, Toyota Corolla pulled up in front of me.

"Miss, are you okay?" A strange man asked.

"Oh, my God! Please help me?" I begged. "Can you get me out of here?"

"Yeah, get in."

I jumped in his car unable to talk because I could not catch my breath; I put the seat all the way back so no one would be able to see me.

"Are you okay? You're bleeding" The Good Samaritan asked, with genuine concern for my safety.

"I got into a fight with my mom and now she's going to call the police." I admitted.

"Well, you're cut pretty bad so if the police see that I don't think you'll be the one going to jail." He said, trying to calm me. "I'm going to stop at the store and get you another shirt, is that okay?"

We stopped at Family Dollar; he went inside and came out with a fresh white t-shirt shirt and a disposable camera.

"I want to take pictures of your face so if something happens you have evidence to protect yourself."

"Why are you helping me?" I asked.

"Because you look like you could use a break." He explained.

"Thank you so much!"

"Where am I taking you?" He asked.

The gracious man dropped me off at a friend's house. She was surprised by my unexpected visit. I tried calling Tony at Jamari's house but they weren't there. I was worried that maybe he was locked up when my mother called the police. The entire day passed before I was able to reach him.

"Where have you been? I've been worried sick!" I told him.

"I'm sorry, Baby Girl. I didn't want to bring heat to my cousin's house so we just went to the bar and had a few drinks until shit died down a little bit. Where are you?"

"I am at Angie's house. Come get me."

"Okay, we're on our way."

He walked through the door with Jamari in tow. I latched onto him, but he pulled away to look at my face.

"Damn! She got you good. Are you okay?" He asked.

"I'm fine." I lied.

"I knew you had hands, but I didn't know you could fight like that for real." He said proudly.

"I don't even know where that came from." I admitted.

"When I saw her hit you, I wanted you to hit her back so bad! After all these years, she finally got what she deserved so don't feel bad about that." He explained.

"It felt good finally standing up for myself, but it hurt me to go there with her. I can't explain it."

"I know. I was so worried about you all day. I am just glad you are safe. You ready to go home?"

"Yes!"

"Thank you for looking out for her Angie."

"No problem Tony." She replied.

24. Darkest Day

Monday morning, Tony returned to work as usual, not wanting to miss any days before his big bonus. I heard a knock at the door, it was Jamari. I opened the door for him; he came in and sat on the sofa.

"What's up?" I asked.

"Tony told me he doesn't want you to worry."

"Worry about what?

"He's locked up." Jamari said sadly.

"Are you serious?" I asked, knowing he was being truthful.

"Yeah, but my dad is about to take me to bail him out right now!"

"What is he charged with?"

"I don't know. Just chill here and be calm. I'm going to get him."

Tony got out the car and I ran to him.

"Are you okay?" I asked.

"I'm good baby. They came and got me from the job. They had

the dogs and everything!" He exclaimed.

"Why?"

"They figured out who I was and where I worked after I ran from them. But they were cool about it. I had a little weed on me so they got me for that, but they were laughing and shit, talking about how fast I was for outrunning the cop who was chasing me."

"So, everything is okay now?"

"Yeah, I gotta go to court but both the charges are misdemeanors."

"Thank God!"

The following weekend, I was sitting outside on the steps, enjoying the June weather when my mom drove by in her car, followed by her fiancé. It scared me because even though he was not on the run from the police anymore, I still was.

He was out trying to scrounge up some money for food because we were broke until his next payday after posting his bond. He rode up on a bicycle with a Little Caesar's pizza and a bag of Thomason's Bar B-Q potato chips in hand. It looked like a feast to my hunger.

"My mom just rolled by."

"Fuck her!"

"I'm not trying to antagonize her." I explained.

"If she rides passed here again I'm going to throw a rock at her fucking car!" He was annoyed.

"Chill out!"

"No! You don't want to antagonize her but she's the one riding passed my house like she is the fucking police! Aint no fear over here baby girl!"

We ate but needed to get out of the house and blow off some steam. The high stress was taking a toll on both of our attitudes. We walked to his cousin Jamari's house to hang out for a while and do something different. The stress of looking over my shoulder for the police made me hypersensitive to everything.

Tony started drinking a few beers and cracking jokes. Something he said set me off and I got up and started walking off as if I actually had some place to go without him.

"Marie!" He called after me. I could hear his footsteps getting closer to me.

"What is wrong with you?" He asked.

"Nothing!" I lied.

"I was only joking! I am trying to have a good day with you and you seem like you're just not into it. I won't keep chasing after you. If this is where you want to be then act like it. I'm not giving up on you but anytime you get mad, you got me walking on eggshells to fix it."

"I'm just worried, okay!" I admitted.

"Worried about what?" He asked.

"That they're gonna come and take me away from you again." I admitted.

"I don't want you to worry about that shit right now. Today, I just want to enjoy our time together."

"I just feel like if they take me away again, I'm going to lose you for good."

"I'm not going anywhere. I am tired of trying to prove that to you! You and me are forever! Don't you get it?" He exclaimed.

I looked at him with a slight smile.

"There you go! That's what I want. Show me those pretty teeth!" We both laughed. "I swear you are lucky I love you like I do or I would've let your ass walk off!" He snickered and wrapped his arm around my shoulders, kissed my forehead and walked with me back to the yard together.

"Y'all good?" Jamari asked.

"Women, can't live with and can't choke em'!" Tony joked.

***

Tony went in the house and came out with a phone in his hand.

"Call your uncle Thomas and find out when your mom is supposed to leave for Florida. See if you can get your I.D. from her before she goes since she has your purse." Tony handed me the phone.

"Hello? Uncle Thomas, it's Marie. Do you know when my mom is leaving for Florida?" I asked when he picked up the phone.

"She is leaving tomorrow."

"Can you get my purse from her? It has my I.D. in it and I need it so I can start working."

"I'm not getting in the middle of whatever you and your mom got going on, Marie."

I could hear my uncle Kevin yelling in the background. He had a reputation for being overly dramatic with a short fuse and lava hot temper.

"That's Marie? Give me the phone!" My Uncle Kevin

demanded.

"Marie!" He yelled into the receiver. "What you did to your mom is fucked up! You flipped on her over a dude and I had to sit here and watch her cry, so just know that when I see Tony, I'm fucking him up on sight!" He yelled.

"Tony doesn't have anything to do with what happened between me and my mom! She hit me first! I tried to walk away!" I attempted to explain.

"Fuck that! That is your mom! I don't give a fuck if she body slammed your ass, you do not put your hands on your mom. I'm going to beat Tony's ass when I see him, just to prove the point." He exclaimed.

"Whose ass are you gonna beat?" A voice grumbled over the line. I turned quickly to see if anyone was standing next to me but I was alone outside.

"Yours, bitch ass nigga!" My uncle screamed.

"We can get it poppin' right now!" Tony yelled into the receiver. "You're talking all this shit but you aint never said shit about the way she does your own niece nigga. You're a pussy! A telephone tough guy!" Tony replied.

"Bitch, come over here and I'll show you exactly how big of a pussy I am!"

"Stop it! You guys are friends!" I yelled.

"We stopped being friends when I found out he was fucking my niece!" Kevin lied.

"Nah, we stopped being friends when I figured out you were a deadbeat dad who left his baby momma for dead!" Tony spat back at him.

"Tony! Hang up the phone!" I pleaded.

"Listen to your girl, Tony!" Kevin antagonized.

"Oh, I'm hanging up the phone but just know that when I put this bitch down, I'm coming!" He warned.

"Let's go!" Kevin challenged.

Before I could blink, Tony ran out the door and was nearly half way up the street with Jamari and I in tow. He was going so fast I could not catch up. I was at a brisk jog, nearly out of breath and before I knew it, there was so much space between us, I could barely see them. I bent the corner on the street my uncle lived on, from a distance, I could see group of people standing outside of his apartment.

I ran to see what was going on and just as I got there, I saw Tony swing and crack Kevin in the face. His head turned with the loud punch, but he ate it. They traded blows for a few moments but Kevin hit him with a hard blow to the face and his knees buckled a little bit. Taking full advantage of the situation, Kevin grabbed Tony and slammed him to the ground. They wrestled for the top for a few seconds but Kevin had the advantage. I tried pushing him off Tony but he would not budge, he just continued to throw punches. I didn't know what to do but react. I punched my uncle Kevin in the head and it distracted him momentarily while someone grabbed me and pulled me away from the fight. Red and blue lights flashed as the cops began to arrive and Kevin scattered. Tony and Jamari ran up the stairs after him, I followed.

Seeing the police there, I knew that if Tony was caught, he was going to jail. As I got up the stairs, Jamari was in my Uncle Thomas's apartment trying to fight him. I pushed him out of the apartment and Thomas shut and locked the door behind me. Tony was trying to get into the neighbor's apartment where he saw Kevin run into, kicking at the door. I pushed his sweaty body against the wall and grabbed his face with both hands.

"Baby, we gotta go! The police are here!" I yelled at him finally able to get his attention. He handed me his keys, grabbed my face and kissed me on the lips before he ran down the stairs. I walked, feeling confident that he would outrun the police as he did a few days earlier.

I walked back to Jamari's house and his dad drove me back to my uncle's apartment to try to find Tony and Jamari. There was a large group of people standing on the bridge next to the apartment, looking down. I got out the car and walked the bridge.

"What happened?" I asked a woman standing there.

"Some man was running from the police. They're going in with divers they think he's in the water!" She exclaimed.

I smirked. *He is not in that water. He can't swim. He is already on his way home!*

I got back in the car and we continued to drive around looking for them. Finally, we gave up and he took me home.

"He's probably already at the house, waiting, cuz I have his house key!" I reasoned aloud.

When I got home, he wasn't there and I started to get worried because a lot of time had passed. I walked to the bridge near our house hoping to run into him on his way home.

I stood on the bridge and tried to see out into the darkness. *He has got to be okay, right? God, please let him be okay! Let him be home when I get there.*

To my disappointment, Tony still was not home but it was too soon to hang up hope. I laid his white t-shirt, key chain and watch on the sofa for him. I tried to busy myself with a shower so I wouldn't go into a panic. *He will be back by the time I'm out! Just breathe!*

The water was cold but I needed to calm my nerves.

"God, I know sometimes I ask you for too much, but please hear me now and bring him home to me, safely. I will not ask you for another thing as long as I live. Please! Amen." I reasoned with God.

Just as I finished my prayer, I heard a loud banging on the bottom door of the apartment. I jumped out the shower and grabbed my towel. I went to the window to see if it was Tony. It wasn't. To my surprise and dismay, it was my uncle David and his girlfriend. My heart sank.

I ran to the door and outside on the top of the stairs, in my towel.

"David! Why are you here?" I asked.

"Marie..." I could see fear etched across his face as he hesitated. "They pulled a body out of the water and they think it's Tony."

I dropped my towel and stood outside in the night air naked, screaming at the top of my lungs. David grabbed my towel and pushed me in the house trying to cover me up. I hit his chest and cried as he held onto me. "You're lying! You're lying! Tell me you're lying! Tell me it's not him!" I demanded.

"Marie, I wouldn't lie to you about something like this. Put on some clothes so we can go to the hospital." He gently demanded.

I raced in the house and put on the first thing I could find. A pair of Tony's sweat pants and the white t-shirt he had been wearing all day with his house shoes. No bra, no underwear, my hair was dripping wet but I didn't care. I needed to know if it was him.

My knees were so weak I could barely stand. Before getting in the car, I sat on the side of the driveway rocking back and forth. *It is not him! David is wrong! It's not him! It's not him! Please, God don't let it be him! I'll do anything you want! Please!!!*

The moment we arrived at the hospital they ushered us back to a private waiting area. I could not stop crying or hoping they were wrong. I sat in the chair waiting for a doctor to come speak with us and finally he did.

"Did he have any tattoos?" He asked.

"Yes! He has a tattoo of his name on his left arm!" I exclaimed. The doctor's face was blank and I could not tell what was coming but I felt my emotions building and ready to erupt like a volcano.

"Just tell me already! Is it him?" I asked, agitated.

"It's him." He said softly.

I slide out of my chair onto the floor screaming at the top of my lungs.

"Take me! Please take me instead!" I begged. "He can't leave me here!" I screamed, kicked and flailed my body across the waiting room floor. "Why! Why God? No! No! I need him! I can't live without him! Take me!"

A nurse entered the waiting room and tried to calm me down. Her tender touch only made my painful sobs, deepen.

"Can I see him?" I begged. "You don't know what he looks

like; you could have the wrong person!" I hollered.

"I will let you see him but you have to be calm and you have to promise not to touch him." She urged.

"I promise!"

It's not him! It's not him! It is not him! I told myself, walking down the cold, hospital hallway with the nurse holding me up. She pulled back the curtain and I saw the bottom of his feet. My knees buckled, but she caught me and walked me closer to his lifeless body.

He laid there still. He looked as though he was sleeping with a thin white sheet covering his body and a blue brace stabilizing his head. His bottom lip was busted but otherwise he looked peaceful.

"You can touch his hand." The nurse said.

Somebody please wake me up from this nightmare!

"You are my soul mate, you weren't supposed to leave me! How do I live without you now? Who am I without you? I love you so much. I will never stop loving you. Please, wake up! Don't leave me!" I whispered to him through agonizing tears.

"It's time to go. You can kiss his forehead if you like." The nurse explained.

I bent towards him, and kissed his forehead one last time.

"I'll never stop loving you for as long as I live. I promise. Goodbye my love."

I left a piece of my soul in the hospital that night. My eyes were burning from crying so hard, I did not have any tears left. I let them dry on my face knowing he would never be there to wipe them away again.

Once I was home, our apartment felt empty and cold. I wrapped myself in a blanket and laid in bed hoping I would wake up to find out that I was having a horrible nightmare and he would be there to comfort me.

A panic attack in the middle of the night woke me out of my sleep, I reached for him and he wasn't there. When I could finally breathe, I screamed at the top of my lungs into his pillow.

How could you do this to me God? Why did you take him from me? Why didn't you take me instead? Why did I call my uncle's house? Why did I tell him to run? Why didn't I follow behind him? Why didn't I jump in the water when the lady said that the divers were going in after him? Why didn't I believe her? Why, God? What did I do that was so wrong that you would take the only person who loves me? Why? Haven't I been through enough pain? Bring him back to me! Please bring him back! Take me! I HATE you for taking him from me! Please, take me instead!

Days were blurry and I was numb. Food did not taste the same anymore so I barely ate. I wanted nothing to do with the outside world, all I wanted was him. I did not want to leave the apartment we shared because a part of me hoped that he would walk in one day and say, "I was just joking baby girl!" I did not want to laugh or have fun nor do anything that would make me miss him any less. I wanted to feel his presence all around me, every minute, for as long as I could. I dressed in his clothes, I listened to songs that reminded me of him, and I read and re-read his letters just to hear his words in my head. I feared the day would come when I would forget the sound of his voice.

My grandmother came to visit me.

"Honey, you got to get out this bed." She whispered softly. "I know you're hurting but you gotta keep living life, that's what Tony would want you to do."

"But he's not here Grandma! How do I live without him?" I cried.

"You just do baby. Every day you find a little bit of strength." She explained as she ran her fingers through my uncombed hair.

"When was the last time you ate something?" She asked.

I didn't answer.

"You gotta eat baby. Come on!" She used what little strength she had to pull me up. Her tender touch made me fall apart in her arms and she hugged me tight.

"He's never coming back to me Grandma! It hurts so bad!" I sobbed.

"I know it hurts! Let it out! Let it all out!"

FOR MY READERS

Tony's death changed me forever. I didn't know if I would ever make it through the intense pain and sadness I felt from losing him. Every day, the simplest tasks seemed overwhelming. I clung to my Grandmother who became my lifeline and somehow, I mustered up just enough courage to make it through, one day at a time. I still remember the crushing guilt I felt the very first time I laughed at a joke after he died. I became numb to everyone and everything around me, except my Grandmother. She breathed life back into me over time. Our bond grew an unbreakable strength as she watched me struggle to find my new normal. I owe my life to her.

I decided to write this book to shed some light on juvenile incarceration, sexual abuse and neglectful parenting, to which, the after-effects are infinite and devastating. As a survivor, I have a first-hand account of the daily struggle to live a normal life.

Early childhood and teenage years are pivotal in the development of children and play a significant role as to who and what they will become as adults. I do not believe that any child is beyond repair and placing them in a concrete box to punish them for their actions, significantly alters their progress and ability to be fully rehabilitated.

By most American standards, I have grown into an exceptional woman. I have a career that I dedicate most of my time too, I own property, I pay taxes and donate to several organizations in an effort to give back to the community. However, the time I spent as a prisoner to the Juvenile Justice System caused me to create a prison within myself that I hopelessly try to escape.

Getting close to people seems to be the most difficult for me. Somehow, even those that I love desperately, I continue to keep at a distance, only allowing them in so far before I shut down or pull away. I have found solace in being alone and yet still feel a longing desire to connect with people.

The sexual and physical abuse I withstood, damaged my ability to appreciate uninitiated physical touch, such as a simple hug. It baffles me how something so small, could cause such an intense level of anxiety within me. I have undergone excessive therapy and I have made tremendous breakthroughs because of it. Nevertheless, brokenness lingered within me and hindered me from finding a true happiness within myself.

Over time, I learned to accept myself for everything that I am and all that I am not. I used to feel ashamed of my story until I found the beauty in it. We are all one decision away from a very different life. By all accounts, I was a statistic and my life should've been very different from what it is today, but God's plan for me was different. *Why?* That is a question that I often ask myself. I wasn't so special, but what was special within me was my determination to rise up and fight through whatever circumstances are stacked up against me. Sometimes I win, other times, I learn.

Unfortunately for most young girls, their story does not turn out the same way. I attribute my success to Tony's presence in my life and while some do not fully understand that due to the unconventional nature of our relationship, it is my truth. Despite our age difference, he was a blessing to me. His vision for my future was very clear; he encouraged me to become my best self and even in his death, I fear his disappointment. He was a source of hope and strength for me, then and now. While I do not advocate for these types of unconventional relationships and fully understand that my situation was unique, I also believe that all young people need unconditional love and if they do not receive it from their parents, they will seek it out. So many young women grow up lost without that love. They end up being with men that prey upon their low self-esteem, feed their addiction for attention and love, and then mentally, physically, and sexually abuse them. Before long, they become victims of their own poor choices and desperation.

We have the power to step in and step up for the next generation. We have a duty to become the people we needed when we were young. We can end the relentless cycle of unloved, unwanted and unprotected children in our communities, one child at a time. Your constant presence alone can be enough to influence a child's life forever. I urge you to get to know the children around you and become involved in their lives as much as possible. Be someone they can trust. Listen to understand them. Having your ear, may give them the courage to come forward if they are being abused, it could mean one less child being harmed or damaged.

I encourage you to look beneath the actions of "bad" children to find the root causes. Do not allow yourself to be shut out or pushed away because they are testing your ability to stick around. Be an example that they can look up too and if you know of a child who is suffering from sexual or physical abuse, speak up! Protect them no matter the cost because it is the right thing to do.

Placing a child into the Juvenile Justice System is not always the answer. I know firsthand, how flawed our system is. What they deem to be "help," usually ends up creating many other issues that can take a lifetime to heal.

***

If you are reading this and you have suffered and survived any of the things I discuss in this book, I implore you to find help. I know it can seem like the weight of the world is on your shoulders and there is nowhere to turn, but when you are at your lowest point in life, so far down that you have to look up, to see the bottom...
That is when God steps in!

Understand that there is a lesson in your pain and struggle. Fight for your own survival. You can do it! God will send the help you need to push through, just be willing to accept the help he gives you, in whatever form it comes. You may not believe it, but you are someone's blessing! Never forget how valuable you are even if the people you love the most, forget to show you your worth.

So many people had my story all mapped out for me. What I was going to become, where I was going to be, etc., but with God's grace and my own strong determination, I continue to rise. I am not going to tell you that it is easy because that would be a lie. When the deck is set against you, you may have to work twice as hard to get half as far, but it will be worth it. Don't let other people's opinions or your current circumstances hold you back from going out into the world and creating the life you want for yourself. It is within your reach and not something that you just see on television. Love yourself enough to dream impossible dreams, put in the leg-work to make them happen and watch them manifest themselves before your eyes.

***

As far as my story goes, there were a lot of things left out for various reasons, such as the depths of my struggles during my incarceration, my parents back-story and more. One thing I want my readers to know is that as troubled as my childhood was, my parents also did not have an easy life growing up and while that doesn't excuse some of their behaviors, it has given me a better understanding as to why my childhood was so difficult. It is a cycle of brokenness that is passed on through generations. I am determined to break that cycle for the future generations of our family and do my part to positively impact the lives of as many young people as I possibly can.

When it comes to my bi-polar disorder, I do not encourage anyone that is suffering with mental health issues, to stop taking their medication. It was the right thing for ME and over the years I have struggled to learn new ways to cope with this disorder. It has cost me career opportunities, friendships, and relationships but still, I fight a daily battle to lead a normal life. There are days when it is a struggle just to get out of bed and other days when I have more energy than ten men combined and I think I can conquer the world. I do my best to find a happy medium with the help of some really, amazing people who support and motivate me. It is that supportive group of individuals that help me to remain strong and push through on my worst days.

Acknowledgments

I have spent over a decade of my life shaping myself into the woman I wanted to be. I was blessed to find a sister along my journey that has loved and guided me throughout my growing pains. She is a source of strength for me, a mentor and an incredible woman with whom I have grown to love with an unbelievable intensity. Thank you, Crystal.

To Fred, I attribute so much of my growth as a woman to you. Thank you for being my voice of reason and clarity. 8412

Ben, Mrs. Joanne, Isabel, Mr. Fred, Mary, Meechie, Bruce, Walter, Moca, Willie, Nekole, Izak, Tia, Lela, Rebecca, Amber, Jennifer, Lori, Blue and Wayne. I thank you from the bottom of my heart for your wisdom, guidance, love and support. This book would not have been possible without you. I am forever grateful for your presence in my life.

I owe a special thank you to a very good friend that gave me the motivation I needed to finally finish this book. Joey, thank you for your encouragement and continued support. You are an incredible mind.

I would also like to thank my family for their support. While some of you may find this book difficult to read, I hope you understand that it is only a reflection of my truth from a portion of my life and does not reflect how our relationships may have grown since then. I love you all.

To my mother... We have grown apart and come back together countless times over the years but what always remains is my undying love for you. Your pain has always been my own. In the deepest depths of my soul I regret the moment I ever raised my hand to you. No matter how much I may have felt justified in my actions at the time, I am sorry Mom. I know that if you could go back in time, you would've done so many things differently. I hope you understand that this book was not written in an attempt to hurt you, only to speak my truth. I love you forever.

Lastly, my father. Your presence and absence in my life had such a profound impact on who I have become. No matter what, you will always have a special place in my heart. Thank you.

I am not perfect, failure is a part of life but we only truly fail when we give up and stop trying. I will continue to grow through it all with the love and support of my inner circle.

Thank you for reading.

THE RUG IS LIFTED...

For more information about the author, upcoming books or events, visit her website:

WWW.LMARIEWILLIAMS.COM